BIOGRAPHY SAWYER
Gallop-Goodman, Gerda.
Diane Sawyer

DIANE SAWYER

DIANE SAWYER

Gerda Gallop-Goodman

MAR   2002

CHELSEA HOUSE PUBLISHERS
PHILADELPHIA

Frontispiece: Journalist Diane Sawyer has made a lasting impression as a reporter and anchor for a number of news shows, including *60 Minutes*, *PrimeTime Live*, and *Good Morning America*.

Chelsea House Publishers
EDITOR IN CHIEF Sally Cheney
DIRECTOR OF PRODUCTION Kim Shinners
PRODUCTION MANAGER Pamela Loos
ART DIRECTOR Sara Davis
EDITOR LeeAnne Gelletly
PRODUCTION EDITOR Diann Grasse
LAYOUT 21st Century Publishing and Communications, Inc.

The Chelsea House World Wide Web address is
http://www.chelseahouse.com

First Printing
1 3 5 7 9 8 6 4 2

CIP applied for ISBN 0-7910-6316-X (HC)/0-7910-6317-8(PB)

CONTENTS

WOMEN of ACHIEVEMENT

Jane Addams
SOCIAL WORKER

Madeleine Albright
STATESWOMAN

Marian Anderson
SINGER

Susan B. Anthony
WOMAN SUFFRAGIST

Joan of Arc
FRENCH SAINT AND HEROINE

Clara Barton
AMERICAN RED CROSS FOUNDER

Rachel Carson
BIOLOGIST AND AUTHOR

Cher
SINGER AND ACTRESS

Cleopatra
QUEEN OF EGYPT

Hillary Rodham Clinton
FIRST LADY AND ATTORNEY

Katie Couric
JOURNALIST

Diana, Princess of Wales
HUMANITARIAN

Emily Dickinson
POET

Elizabeth Dole
POLITICIAN

Amelia Earhart
AVIATOR

Gloria Estefan
SINGER

Jodie Foster
ACTRESS AND DIRECTOR

Ruth Bader Ginsburg
SUPREME COURT JUSTICE

Katherine Graham
PUBLISHER

Helen Hayes
ACTRESS

Mahalia Jackson
GOSPEL SINGER

Helen Keller
HUMANITARIAN

**Ann Landers/
Abigail Van Buren**
COLUMNISTS

Barbara McClintock
BIOLOGIST

Margaret Mead
ANTHROPOLOGIST

Julia Morgan
ARCHITECT

Toni Morrison
AUTHOR

Grandma Moses
PAINTER

Lucretia Mott
WOMAN SUFFRAGIST

Sandra Day O'Connor
SUPREME COURT JUSTICE

Rosie O'Donnell
ENTERTAINER AND COMEDIAN

Georgia O'Keeffe
PAINTER

Eleanor Roosevelt
DIPLOMAT AND HUMANITARIAN

Wilma Rudolph
CHAMPION ATHLETE

Diane Sawyer
JOURNALIST

Elizabeth Cady Stanton
WOMAN SUFFRAGIST

Martha Stewart
ENTREPRENEUR

Harriet Beecher Stowe
AUTHOR AND ABOLITIONIST

Barbra Streisand
ENTERTAINER

Amy Tan
AUTHOR

Elizabeth Taylor
ACTRESS AND ACTIVIST

Mother Teresa
HUMANITARIAN AND
RELIGIOUS LEADER

Barbara Walters
JOURNALIST

Edith Wharton
AUTHOR

Phillis Wheatley
POET

Oprah Winfrey
ENTERTAINER

"REMEMBER THE LADIES"

MATINA S. HORNER

"Remember the Ladies." That is what Abigail Adams wrote to her husband John, then a delegate to the Continental Congress, as the Founding Fathers met in Philadelphia to form a new nation in March of 1776. "Be more generous and favorable to them than your ancestors. Do not put such unlimited power in the hands of the Husbands. If particular care and attention is not paid to the Ladies," Abigail Adams warned, "we are determined to foment a Rebellion, and will not hold ourselves bound by any Laws in which we have no voice, or Representation."

The words of Abigail Adams, one of the earliest American advocates of women's rights, were prophetic. Because when we have not "remembered the ladies," they have, by their words and deeds, reminded us so forcefully of the omission that we cannot fail to remember them. For the history of American women is as interesting and varied as the history of our nation as a whole. American women have played an integral part in founding, settling, and building our country. Some we remember as remarkable women who—against great odds—achieved distinction in the public arena: Anne Hutchinson, who in the 17th century became a charismatic religious leader; Phillis Wheatley, an 18th-century black slave who became a poet; Susan B. Anthony, whose name is synonymous with the 19th-century women's rights movement, and who led the struggle to enfranchise women; and in the 20th century, Amelia Earhart, the first woman to cross the Atlantic Ocean by air.

These extraordinary women certainly merit our admiration, but other women, "common women," many of them all but forgotten, should also be recognized for their contributions to American thought and culture. Women have been community builders; they have founded schools and formed voluntary associations to help those in need; they have assumed the major responsibility for rearing children, passing on from one generation to the next the values that keep a culture alive. These and innumerable other contributions, once ignored, are now being recognized by scholars, students, and the public. It is exciting and gratifying that a part of our history that was hardly acknowledged a few generations ago is now being studied and brought to light.

In recent decades, the field of women's history has grown from obscurity to a politically controversial splinter movement to academic respectability, in many cases mainstreamed into such traditional disciplines as history, economics, and psychology. Scholars of women, both female and male, have organized research centers at such prestigious institutions as Wellesley College, Stanford University, and the University of California. Other notable centers for women's studies are the Center for the American Woman and Politics at the Eagleton Institute of Politics at Rutgers University; the Henry A. Murray Research Center for the Study of Lives, at Radcliffe College; and the Women's Research and Education Institute, the research arm of the Congressional Caucus on Women's Issues. Other scholars and public figures have established archives and libraries, such as the Schlesinger Library on the History of Women in America, at Radcliffe College, and the Sophia Smith Collection, at Smith College, to collect and preserve the written and tangible legacies of women.

From the initial donation of the Women's Rights Collection in 1943, the Schlesinger Library grew to encompass vast collections documenting the manifold accomplishments of American women. Simultaneously, the women's movement in general and the academic discipline of women's studies in particular also began with a narrow definition and gradually expanded their mandate. Early causes, such as woman suffrage and social reform, abolition, and organized labor were joined by newer concerns, such as the history of women in business and the professions and in politics and government; the study of the family; and social issues such as health policy and education.

Women, as historian Arthur M. Schlesinger, jr., once pointed out, "have constituted the most spectacular casualty of traditional history. They have made up at least half the human race, but you could never tell that by looking at the books historians write." The new breed of historians is remedying that omission. They have written books about immigrant women and about working-class women who struggled for survival in cities and about black women who met the challenges of life in rural areas. They are telling the stories of women who, despite the barriers of tradition and economics, became lawyers and doctors and public figures.

The women's studies movement has also led scholars to question traditional interpretations of their respective disciplines. For example, the study of war has traditionally been an exercise in military and political analysis, an examination of strategies planned and executed by men. But scholars of women's history have pointed out that wars have also been periods of tremendous change and even opportunity for women, because the very absence of men on the home front enabled them to expand their educational, economic, and professional activities and to assume leadership in their homes.

The early scholars of women's history showed a unique brand of courage in choosing to investigate new subjects and take new approaches to old ones. Often, like their subjects, they endured criticism and even ostracism by their academic colleagues. But their efforts have unquestionably been worthwhile, because with the publication of each new study and book another piece of the historical patchwork is sewn into place, revealing an increasingly comprehensive picture of the role of women in our rich and varied history.

Such books on groups of women are essential, but books that focus on the lives of individuals are equally indispensable. Biographies can be inspirational, offering their readers the example of people with vision who have looked outside themselves for their goals and have often struggled against great obstacles to achieve them. Marian Anderson, for instance, had to overcome racial bigotry in order to perfect her art and perform as a concert singer. Isadora Duncan defied the rules of classical dance to find true artistic freedom. Jane Addams had to break down society's notions of the proper role for women in order to create new social situations, notably the settlement house. All of these women had to come to terms both with themselves and with the world in which they lived. Only then could they move ahead as pioneers in their chosen callings.

Biography can inspire not only by adulation but also by realism. It helps us to see not only the qualities in others that we hope to emulate, but also, perhaps, the weaknesses that made them "human." By helping us identify with the subject on a more personal level they help us feel that we, too, can achieve such goals. We read about Eleanor Roosevelt, for instance, who occupied a unique and seemingly enviable position as the wife of the president. Yet we can sympathize with her inner dilemma; an inherently shy woman, she had to force herself to live a most public life in order to use her position to benefit others. We may not be able to imagine ourselves having the immense poetic talent of Emily Dickinson, but from her story we can understand the challenges faced by a creative woman who was expected to fulfill many family responsibilities. And though few of us will ever reach the level of athletic accomplishment displayed by Wilma Rudolph or Babe Zaharias, we can still appreciate their spirit, their overwhelming will to excel.

A biography is a multifaceted lens. It is first of all a magnification, the intimate examination of one particular life. But at the same time, it is a wide-angle lens, informing us about the world in which the subject lived. We come away from reading about one life knowing more about the social, political, and economic fabric of the time. It is for this reason, perhaps, that the great New England essayist Ralph Waldo Emerson wrote in 1841, "There is properly no history: only biography." And it is also why biography, and particularly women's biography, will continue to fascinate writers and readers alike.

Diane Sawyer and coanchor Charles Gibson survey their new studio for Good Morning America. *The show's producers recruited Diane to its new star anchor position in 1999 to help boost its low ratings. They also revamped the show's image by relocating to a studio overlooking New York's Times Square.*

1

RISE AND SHINE

It's 3:30 A.M. Most people are asleep . . . except maybe policemen, bakers, and morning news anchors.

"You get up in the morning and think, 'This [schedule] is impossible. No human can do this,'" says Diane Sawyer, the latest morning star of the ABC network. But then something gives her hope: "As long as I can sleep on weekends," she says.

Diane's work routine is rigorous: she is up weekdays at 3:30 A.M., at work by 4:00 A.M., and often not home before 11 P.M. Still, television journalist Diane Sawyer looks, as always, alert, energetic, and focused on the task at hand. And that's saying a lot. Diane is a woman who has two major network jobs, a loving husband, and a dazzling social calendar.

Since January 1999, Diane, who has been in broadcast news for more than 20 years, has risen to a new challenge, having taken on what many of her peers consider a punishingly demanding workload. Not only does she coanchor the two-hour, live morning-news show *Good Morning America,* along with Charles Gibson, she also cohosts another program with Gibson—the Wednesday night edition of the newsmagazine *20/20.*

Morning programs like *Good Morning America* are relatively inexpensive to produce; it costs the networks much more to turn out prime-time comedies and dramas. As a result, morning shows can be great moneymakers, capable of bringing in $500 million in ad revenues to the networks, according to the show business magazine *Variety.* Also, the commercials aired during station breaks in the morning can promote other network programs.

However, the ratings for ABC's *Good Morning America* had run a roller coaster ride over the past decades. During much of the 1980s, it had been the most-watched morning program. Even as late as 1994, it was still neck and neck with NBC's *Today* show. ABC, the youngest of the three major networks (American Broadcasting Company, or ABC; Columbia Broadcasting System, or CBS; and National Broadcasting Company, or NBC), had gotten a relatively late start in the "morning-show race." But soon after *Good Morning America* debuted in 1975, featuring actor David Hartman as its anchor, it set new standards for morning programming. Unlike today's format, the earlier version of the show focused mostly on features and entertainment, with minimal emphasis on news.

At first *Good Morning America* overtook NBC's *Today.* To get back in the running *Today* changed its format, adopting cozy sets, creating more features, and focusing on the chemistry between its cohosts— many of the same elements that had worked for *Good Morning America.* Over the next 20 years, the two shows would constantly vie for supremacy in the television rating wars.

By the mid-1990s, *Today,* with Katie Couric as its star, had settled into the top spot of morning shows. Meanwhile, *Good Morning America,* featuring Charles Gibson and Joan Lunden, was suffering, continuing

A poster for the NBC morning news program Today, *starring Matt Lauer and Katie Couric.* Good Morning America *producers expected that the addition of Diane Sawyer would help the show compete with* Today *and CBS's* This Morning.

to lose viewers to NBC. In 1995 *Good Morning America* was placed under control of the news division, after many years of being under the direction of the entertainment division, and the show's focus soon drifted and became stale. So when longtime coanchor Joan Lunden was ushered out in 1997, no one appeared to be an obvious successor. Then Gibson left as well, and the show's new anchor team, consisting of newcomers Lisa McRee and Kevin Newman, showed little chemistry. Soon *Good Morning America*'s viewer ratings not only lagged behind *Today*'s ratings, but also had even dropped behind CBS's usually third-ranked *This Morning.*

Ad revenues for the highly profitable morning time period kept shrinking, and ABC saw the need for drastic action. Rumors of an impending change had been floating for weeks when finally the ax fell: host Lisa McRee learned on a Sunday afternoon that she was not to come to work on Monday. "The show was a mess," McRee told *Time* magazine. "It wasn't fun to work on, and it wasn't fun to watch."

In an effort to save *Good Morning America* from faltering so badly in the ratings, ABC called in Diane Sawyer, along with Charles Gibson. Although Gibson had anchored *Good Morning America* from 1987 to 1998, he had recently left the show to concentrate on the prime-time show *20/20*.

ABC News president David Westin acknowledged that solving the problems required extreme measures. "The show simply was not getting better fast enough. I concluded that we needed to make a quantum leap rather than do it incrementally." Television broadcast journalist Connie Chung reportedly turned down the job as McRee's replacement. Then ABC lured Diane Sawyer to team up with Charles Gibson for only "a few months" (enough time to right the ship and find permanent successors).

Good Morning America executive producer Shelley Ross made the final plea to Diane. She said, "I thought I was sitting on the best-kept secret of the decade. I knew the Diane Sawyer that the rest of the world is only now getting to see. In addition to being the best journalist out there, she was a warm and funny person who was wonderful to be around. She is the kind of person who will get down on the floor with you at 3 A.M., rewriting a script . . . she is a good soldier." With Gibson already on board, ABC News president David Westin told Diane, "Charlie will come back if you'll come back." "And there it is," Diane said. "If it had gone on long, we would have come to our senses."

Ross further recalled how she convinced Diane to

come on board. "I was actually on an airplane," said Ross. "I remember the pilot had just said we were over Kansas when I thought that this would be a really great move for her. Not just for the show, but for her."

Diane recalled the same event, "It was Christmas Eve (1998) and she [Ross] called and said, 'I'm over Kansas, and it seems like a good idea that you come to the morning [show] with me.' The two women laughed, enjoying the moment as they completed the agreement over the phone. By the end of the day, ABC had also recruited Charles Gibson.

Gibson says that the show had gotten "dumbed down" in order to attract younger viewers. He noted that ABC needed to bring in a "megastar" of Diane Sawyer's stature to compete against *Today's* Katie Couric.

Sawyer and Gibson are not being paid extra for coanchoring *Good Morning America*. Diane Sawyer states she agreed to cohost *Good Morning America* out of loyalty to ABC. She had already established herself as a star at CBS before she moved to ABC in 1989 to coanchor *PrimeTime Live* with Sam Donaldson. (Although she helped launch that show, it was later combined with newsmagazine *20/20*). As of 1999 Diane was making $7 million per year and had nothing to prove and little to gain by leaving prime time (the time period when a television audience is the largest) in an attempt to rescue a flailing morning show.

Nevertheless, the thought of saving the program intrigued Diane: "I love it when the whole foundation starts to shift, and everybody's trying to figure out what's going on. That's what we're all doing. You have a sense that something powerful and new is beginning and you are right in the middle of it. I love it."

"We're not going to change the ratings or the competitive relationship with the *Today* show," Diane said. The idea was to get the show back on course and

ABC News president David Westin (center) speaks with executive associates of the media. As president, Westin has made a number of successful moves regarding ABC News shows, including bringing Diane Sawyer to Good Morning America *on the strength of her shows' viewer ratings.*

"more connected to the rest of the news division." Diane said she took on *Good Morning America* to help out ABC News chief David Westin, and denied that she moved to *Good Morning America* because of any unhappiness with her role at *PrimeTime Live*.

Above all, Diane wants to do a good job as anchor on *Good Morning America*. "We want to be the people, of course, about whom you say, 'I'd like to have coffee with them in the morning,'" she says. "I want people to wake up and say, 'I really want to know what Charlie Gibson and Diane Sawyer can tell me this morning.'"

Even though the morning news team was supposed to be anchoring for only a few months until new coanchors could be found, the pairing has happily lasted much longer. The search for talent has not produced a sparkling replacement, and Diane, although "not a morning person," continues to set her alarm for 3:30 A.M.

five mornings a week. She often works until 7:00 P.M. or later. And she manages on a couple of week-nights to go out with her husband of 13 years, director Mike Nichols. How does she do it? Even renowned television journalist Barbara Walters has described Diane's grueling routine as "completely beyond my comprehension."

Thus far, *Good Morning America*'s ratings are on the upswing, with the show's numbers managing to close the gap somewhat between it and its main competition, NBC's *Today*. In fact, by the last week in January 2000, *Good Morning America* had seen its best ratings in more than two years, indicating that Gibson and Sawyer were drawing in the viewers. *Good Morning America* earned a rating of 4.3—a 30-percent increase above the 3.3 rating it earned during the same time period in 1999. This rating represents 4.8 million viewers. Meanwhile, *Today*'s 5.6 rating represents 6.4 million viewers. Since the debut of Diane Sawyer and Charles Gibson as a team in January 1999, the number of *Good Morning America*'s viewers grew by 1.1 million. During the same time frame, the *Today* audience grew by about 454,000. While a wide gap still remains, the presence of Diane Sawyer and Charles Gibson on the show has given it much needed stability.

"How we start in the morning at ABC matters to the strength of the whole network," Diane said. "It ripples throughout the day."

Diane, a former beauty queen whose looks are a cornerstone of her success, is perhaps the most enigmatic woman on television. She is described as easy-going, passionate, driven, retiring, earnest, and shy.

Diane has loyal friends in high positions as well as critics. Now that she is entrenched in the rescue of *Good Morning America*, speculation over her motives has only intensified. Diane has said she took the job simply because her bosses wanted her to help out. But some insiders believe that Diane has negotiated a deal with

Diane has worked alongside and sometimes substituted for veteran news anchor Peter Jennings (right) on ABC's World News Tonight. *Insiders predict that Diane may take Jennings's position on the program after he retires.*

ABC News chief David Westin to save *Good Morning America* in exchange for stepping into Peter Jennings' anchor spot on ABC's evening news program, should he retire soon.

Still, some of her friends counter that Diane simply wanted to show another side of herself by doing "soft and feel-good" morning TV. Don Hewitt, executive producer of CBS' *60 Minutes*, where Diane spent four years as the first female correspondent, has said she simply "likes the idea of coming to the rescue."

Lesley Stahl, a *60 Minutes'* journalist and friend of Diane's since the 1970s, says, "Some people can't believe she is doing this just because she is having fun and, at the same time, helping out the network. That's totally in character for her. She's genuinely a kind person who knows precisely the meaning of friendship."

Diane is passionate about journalism. Often accused of overreporting, she edits and edits again until technicians are nearly driven to the breaking point. "They love her," one of her associates says, "but she drives them a little crazy."

Husband Mike Nichols agrees with this assessment of Sawyer's perfection: "She is so obsessed with the quality of the work that to dwell even a little bit on her appearance would be shameful to her."

Diane professes that, as she gets older, she is less obsessed with the traditional signs and trappings of success. Even becoming the nation's first female anchor seemed unimportant to Diane. "There was a time when that was the only way to nudge the world," Diane said. "But that isn't true anymore. There isn't the audience at that hour anymore. Sure, there would be a symbolic achievement to be the first female anchor, but it would really be just that—a symbol."

Diane has a highly developed sense of humor about herself and her career. "I want the theme parks, that's what I'm after [referring to Disney, ABC's parent company]. That's my secret, why I'm doing all this. I want a Diane ride. People go into a dark tunnel and come out finding the whole thing utterly inscrutable. Now that would be fun."

Indeed, Diane Sawyer has risen to the top with a formidable blend of smarts, drive, and earnestness. "I considered myself so lucky to have been given this gift, to be able to come in without having paid the kind of dues that a lot of them [other reporters] did," Diane has said. "I was respectful of it and thought, 'Well, I guess I have to do the grunge work, and I'll do it harder than anyone else.'"

Diane's manner is both authoritative and appealing. She is willing to move between tabloid journalist and "legitimate" journalist, producing diligent reporting pieces along with insightful and entertaining celebrity interviews, such as covering the Iranian hostage crises in the 1970s and interviewing pop superstar Michael Jackson in the 1980s.

Diane has attributed the success of her interviews to conscientiousness. "I suppose my method of work—if you can call it that—is to overcompensate. I always read the extra book, I get there earlier than anybody else, and I make those extra phone calls." And Diane has won over the television audience and industry insiders as well. Her distinctive personality has helped *Good Morning America* and *PrimeTime Live*, where she was coanchor, move toward unqualified success and produce millions of dollars in profits for ABC.

It has been said of Diane Sawyer that she often gets things the way she wants them, but without trampling on others. She is well liked by all in the industry, and she is shown genuine affection by lower-level workers.

"Diane really went out of her way to put me at ease," said Tony Perkins, who became weatherman for *Good Morning America* in March 1999. "The first morning that I was on the air here, before the show, she called me down from the dressing room, and she had them pump Motown music—she knows I'm a Motown fan—and we all danced. It was like 'American Bandstand' for five or six minutes. It really just calmed my nerves, and made me feel like I was part of the team."

Four major networks have sought out Diane Sawyer because they know she can boost ratings and that viewers remember her. In other words, she has become a "brand name." Viewers admire her for her personality and her talents as an investigative reporter. In addition to an impressive professional résumé, Diane is known for her intelligent, skillful reporting and tenacious coverage of news events. For this she has been rewarded with heavy journalistic assignments, which, at times, were considered a challenge to male colleagues.

In 1994, Diane's new $7-million contract clinched her a spot in an elite group as one of the highest-paid women in broadcast news. She has been characterized as "a girl who is one of the boys" and by her ambition and tenacity. Her sunny outlook, commanding delivery and presence, and sense of teamwork prove to be assets on whatever assignment she has taken. She remains one of the most viable news figures in U.S. television morning and prime-time hours.

One of Good Morning America's most successful anchor teams, Diane Sawyer and Charles Gibson share a light moment on the set. On January 18, 1999, Diane joined the show with Gibson, who before a temporary absence had been the show's coanchor for 11 years.

Before proving her mettle as a journalist, Diane Sawyer shone as a teenage beauty queen, winning the national Junior Miss title in March 1963.

2

A CLASSIC OVERACHIEVER

Lila Diane Sawyer was born December 22, 1945, in the small farm town of Glasgow, Kentucky, to parents Erbon Powers "Tom" Sawyer, a prominent Republican county judge, and Jean W. Dunagan Sawyer, an elementary schoolteacher. Diane's parents were native Kentuckians—both of English and Irish ancestry. Diane's grandfathers were Pappy Jim (her father's father) and Foxy Dunagan (her mother's father). Foxy Dunagan went to work on the farm at age eight to support his family after his father died.

Diane's mother, Jean, was strong and tough-minded, and Diane notes that she gets much of her strength and determination from her mother and the values she taught. Diane has said of her mom, "[She] worked full time, never had help at home of any kind, raised two children and did it all at a time when nobody was celebrating you on the cover of magazines for doing it all."

Tom Sawyer, Diane's father, was intellectual and religious, gentle and reflective. He founded the local Methodist church, where young Diane sang in the choir and played the organ. In his spare time, he composed country music. It is likely that Diane got her love of singing and music from her father.

Diane grew up in her middle-class family in Louisville, Kentucky, at 29 Sterling Road in Sheffield Manor. Sheffield Manor was a subdivision developed by a group of returning World War II veterans. Among them was Diane's father, who was a lawyer before becoming county attorney and then county judge.

Diane remembers Louisville as being a wonderfully secure and happy place to grow up in. She and her sister, Linda, who is two and a half years older, have many fond memories of their early days. "My childhood was very happy," Diane recalls. "My sister and I were very much loved. We were hugged a lot. You're looking at a very hugged woman."

The year of Diane's birth was marked by several historical events. The nation was mourning President Franklin Delano Roosevelt's death, which occurred during his fourth term in office. On April 12, 1945, Vice President Harry S. Truman assumed the presidency. That summer, the United States dropped atomic bombs on Japan on August 6 and 9, 1945, precipitating the end of World War II on August 15, 1945.

As a kid, Diane was the classic overachiever—in her own words, "basically a nerd." Her mother taught at the local elementary school. Diane said, "[My mother] taught me in the third grade. I'll never forget the day she called on me, knowing that I hadn't memorized the Roman numeral for nine." From that point on, Diane explains, she always applied the lesson of being prepared and organized, traits that would characterize her as a professional in later years.

Diane's aunt, Lila Farmer, said of her niece, "Diane was always alert. She was sweet, clever, and funny."

At Seneca High School, in Louisville, Kentucky, Diane was a tall, gangly teen who wore glasses and was, as she described herself, "boringly serious." Her teachers and fellow students have described her as a popular, nice, and friendly girl. They also have said she has a sense of humor and during that time was an accomplished student with exceptional writing skills. According to Diane, "My teachers loved me, which gives you a good idea of what I was like. When I wasn't invited by a boy to the senior prom, my English teacher burst into tears. But I honestly didn't care. I went to see a movie on prom night and had a marvelous time."

Still, Diane mused, "Part of me longed to be like the other girls, to wisecrack, flirt and ride in open cars, screaming with pleasure. But part of me wanted nothing to do with it, and I was something of a loner instead. I was just happy going off by myself or with my group of friends. We called ourselves 'reincarnated transcendentalists' and spent our time reading Emerson and Thoreau down by what I'm sure was a terribly polluted creek." Diane enjoyed spending time with a group of friends who included a few girlfriends and a male friend, Greg Haynes.

Diane blossomed in her late teens. She was voted "Most Likely to Succeed" in her high school class. She was a junior varsity cheerleader, played basketball, and was yearbook editor and a member of the Young Republicans, Pep, Latin, and Quill and Scroll clubs. "It was considered a privilege to participate in cheerleading at my school," recalled Diane in one interview. "My memories of those days are some of my fondest." She also managed to find time to play tennis and enjoyed waterskiing, bowling, and "when time permit[ted] knitting." Diane was also a member of the National Honor Society, the highest honor a student could receive. Faculty members selected students based on high levels of scholarship, character, leadership, and service.

Singing was also a favorite pastime of Diane. "I love to sing almost more than anything else," she has said. "As a teenager, I dreamed of being Julie Andrews. I'd sing along to her records of the *Sound of Music* or *The Boyfriend*. Remember the *Unsinkable Molly Brown* song, 'I Ain't Down Yet?' I used to sing that song over and over along with the recording whenever I was depressed. It was so rowdy and inspirational—it always lifted me to the skies."

Diane's father and mother had high expectations for her and for her older sister, Linda. The girls rose to the occasion, taking elocution, fencing, and singing lessons. There were also piano lessons, ballet, tap, horseback riding, fencing, classical guitar, and children's theater. "The lessons were about [my mother] never having gotten to do those things," Diane said. "She was not steering me in any direction." To expose them to other cultures, the girls also spent a summer in Europe on young people's tours.

Diane was a straight-A student, senior class vice president, the editor in chief of her school paper—the *Arrow*—and an intellectual who loved reading the works of Ralph Waldo Emerson and Henry David Thoreau. Diane learned the art of perfectionism from both of her parents.

Her sister Linda recalls, "Diane was always trying to keep up with the older kids, trying to do tricks on her bike. I remember the intensity of the internal Diane, too. She would memorize poetry even as a young child." Still today, Diane admires her big sister: "It never occurs to me that anyone thinks I'm ladylike. My sister is elegant. I was kind of a parody of elegance. I was always the one to fall down the stairs."

There was a time when Diane saw herself as a "dorky wallflower" compared with Linda, whom Diane recalled, "was so beautiful and so popular." Linda, however, says. "I was just older, that's all. Things that came my way seemed very alluring."

For Diane, who today stands 5'9" inches tall, height was not always an asset. "As a teenager, I was self-conscious about being so tall," she said. "My height

Before graduating from high school and enrolling at Wellesley in 1963, Diane excelled academically and in many of her activities. She received her first journalism experience as editor in chief of her school newspaper.

made me terribly clumsy, and I was always bumping into people and tripping."

She recalled that in ballet school, Linda was given the part of a snowflake while she played a less graceful icicle. Despite her own beauty, Diane to this day downplays her attractiveness. "I've always wanted to look like [actress and singer] Cher," Diane said. "I wanted the straight black hair and one of those coltish bodies."

In a *TV Guide* article, the renowned photographer Francesco Scavullo chose Diane as one of the six most beautiful women on television. He proclaimed Diane Sawyer as "a great beauty and a marvelous newscaster with an incredibly personal style." Diane would cause a stir when she posed on the cover of *Vanity Fair* in 1987 in a fairy tale gown while she was a reporter for the CBS newsmagazine program *60 Minutes.*

"I laugh when people say I'm a fashion plate," said Diane, who happened to appear on *People* magazine's "Best Dressed" list one year. "A couple of times a year I ask my sister to come in from California to pin notes to my clothes telling me what to wear with what."

Diane also recalled trying to keep up with her older sister. Diane and Linda Sawyer often entered beauty pageants. As a teen, Linda was crowned Miss Kentucky and was first runner-up in the Junior Miss pageant. Diane first gained attention when she won the 1963 Kentucky Junior Miss contest at the local Woman's Club Auditorium. Diane's talent demonstration for the pageant was a performance entitled *Five Score Years Ago*, a blend of song, blank verse, and monologue that offered "interpretations of Civil War moods." Diane went on to compete for the national Junior Miss title, and in 1963, despite her long, lanky looks, the blond-haired, blue-eyed 17-year-old managed to snag the crown in the America's Junior Miss pageant. When Diane took the crown, she won a scholarship prize of $11,000 and a trip around the country, along with instructions to wear her sash and crown at all times—even on airplanes.

At the time, Diane recalled telling the judges at the interview that she wanted to join the foreign service when she graduated from college. Little did the judges know, Diane didn't quite know what the foreign service was. She had simply watched a movie and thought it sounded glamorous and sophisticated. For a time, Diane also thought about becoming a

A teenage Diane takes snapshots of the New York City skyline. After winning the title of Junior Miss in 1963, Diane had the opportunity to travel in the United States and Europe.

philosopher, but figured such an occupation was too impractical.

Diane has said of the beauty pageant experience: "I entered America's Junior Miss contest principally because my sister had entered before me. I tended to have no independent judgment in those days. I simply did everything my sister did. When I won, it was a frightening experience." Diane also told one interviewer, "I didn't win just for looks, [college board scores, fitness, poise, and performance in an interview were also considered]. And I wrote an essay comparing the music written during the Civil War . . . the differences between North and South."

Despite her self-professed shyness, Diane traveled 25,000 miles across the country the summer after winning her crown, giving speeches before groups or corporate boards sometimes three times a day. She traveled with a chaperone, who was assigned to accompany her on all visits.

After graduating from Seneca High School, the teen beauty queen used her scholarship money to attend Wellesley College, the renowned women's college in Wellesley, Massachusetts, where Linda was a rising junior. "I was just completely, mindlessly parroting her," Diane told one interviewer. "If she'd become an armed robber or an ax murderer, I might have followed her there too." Wellesley, located on a beautiful, wooded campus near Boston, was started in 1870. Considered a leader in women's education, it boasts prominent alumnae, including former first lady Hillary Rodham Clinton. Eventually, Diane and Linda took off in different directions. Linda lives in Santa Barbara, California, and has worked in marketing. With her husband, physician David Frankel, she has two sons. "I'm much more cautious and traditional than Diane," Linda has said.

Diane's celebrity status didn't help her socially at Wellesley. "I felt self-conscious about being a beauty queen," she has said. "Of course, it didn't help when I arrived at my first college mixer and heard some guy mumble, 'Is that her? She's not so great.' I absolutely froze, then ran back to my dorm and didn't have more than five dates the entire time I was in college."

A self-admitted late bloomer when it comes to love, Diane remained studious. She was a member of Phi Sigma, a literary society, and participated in other campus activities and organizations. She performed in campus theater productions, including the Wellesley Junior Show, and was a member of the Wellesley Blue Notes, a choral group. Diane was even elected vice president of the student body—despite her shyness.

One of Diane's classmates at Wellesley College in Massachusetts was former first lady Hillary Clinton. Diane and Hillary reunite here at an awards breakfast in 1993.

Terribly insecure, young Diane felt inferior and feared being ridiculed by everyone on campus. She worried that people would think she was sophisticated and stuck up. She did not aspire to being labeled sophisticated. "When the other girls were getting packages of Kron chocolates, I was sent turnips, okra, and tomatoes from home—beautifully wrapped," Diane said.

After graduating from Wellesley College in 1967 with a bachelor's degree in English, Diane Sawyer returned home to Louisville where she began her professional career.

In 1967, Diane quickly plunged into her career after graduating from Wellesley and returning to her home in Louisville. Undaunted by the lack of women television journalists at the time, Diane soon found a job as weatherperson for WLKY-TV, an ABC affiliate.

3

THE FAIR-WEATHER MAIDEN

In 1967, Louisville was a prosperous city. It was the top industrial area in the southeast, with manufacturing still the powerful engine of the local economy. The city's largest manufacturers included General Electric, Ford Motor Company, and the tobacco-processing firms Philip Morris, Brown & Williamson, and American Tobacco. And by the mid-1960s, Louisville was ranked one of the top-20 industrial markets.

Yet despite the prosperity of the decade, the city was facing new and unexpected problems. The population was shifting away from the city to the suburbs. The good economic times were giving thousands of residents their first opportunity to own a brand-new home, so they were heading to newly built housing developments in the former cornfields and apple orchards of Jefferson County. Businesses followed suit, as low-rise and high-rise office buildings and shopping malls began to sprout along the expressways.

By the late 1960s, downtown Louisville was struggling. Empty storefronts began appearing along the main street, and parking lots replaced dozens of once-thriving small businesses. Yet by the end of the decade, a downtown renaissance seemed to be under way when construction of the 22-story Galt House (named for a famous 19th-century hotel there) and open plaza began. An urban renewal project cleared blighted areas to make way for the city's medical center, parks, and other attractions.

After college, Diane was uncertain of the direction she wanted to take in her career. She turned to her father for advice, admitting that writing was what she enjoyed most: "I like the power of the word. And working with people. And being in touch with what's happening in the world." He thought that Diane ought to try for a position in television journalism. She knew that it would be tough to break into the profession, however, because there were very few women in television journalism during the late 1960s.

Diane has admitted, "I didn't know anything about journalism. But my dad said: 'Answer these two questions—What do you love, and where is an adventurous place to do it?' The answers were: writing, telling stories of real people. And television seemed bolder and reached more people. That's why I started."

Undaunted, Diane was determined to talk her way into one of the first women's journalist jobs. Despite her lack of experience, Ken Rowland, the news director at Louisville WLKY-TV, an ABC affiliate, hired her.

That first TV job was as the "Weather Maiden" at WLKY-TV. During the late 1960s women were supposed to look pretty, but not say very much on TV newscasts. However, sometimes Diane "showed" her education, lacing her weathercasts with quotes from poets like Emily Dickinson and Charles Baudelaire. "The weather was extraordinarily boring,"

Diane once explained, "so I'd have a quote every now and then."

Diane Sawyer has disparaged her early work, noting in one interview, "I don't know why they didn't fire me after such performances as 'The high today was 65, and the present temperature is 68.' I was so bad at it." Not only did Diane lack a meteorology background, she had poor eyesight. She didn't wear glasses on camera and couldn't tell whether she was looking at the East Coast or West Coast. "I was a terrible weather girl," Diane said. "I was so bad at it."

Despite her blunders, Diane learned a lot from the experience. She often did forecasts and news assignments on location in Louisville. "The first time I went out to shoot film I was a day late for the assignment," Diane recalled. "The second time it was all jerks and knots. My third try was on a hike through the Red River Gorge. I had to stand ahead of the hikers, then stand and shoot until they passed by, then race ahead to be in front of them again. It was really a vigorous hike for me."

Highly ambitious, Diane stayed after hours to learn how to operate the camera and editing equipment. She spent hours talking to her boss, news director Ken Rowland, about being a reporter. Diane was a shy person, but on camera she came across as composed and confident. She worked very hard to improve her presentation and asked for more challenging assignments. Rowland listened to the determined novice and recognized that Diane was bright and passionate about the news. Within two years, she was promoted to the position of full-time news reporter.

One of Diane's first assignments was to interview civil rights supporter and Supreme Court Justice William O. Douglas. However, the assignment proved more challenging than she expected. Diane

Diane's accomplishments as a weatherperson for her station in Louisville landed her other news assignments, such as interviewing Supreme Court Justice William O. Douglas (right), seen here hiking in 1962 with Robert F. Kennedy, U.S. attorney general at the time.

had to trail behind Douglas while he undertook a five-mile hike through the Red River Gorge in the eastern part of Kentucky. The terrain was rugged, yet Diane managed to carry her own camera and equipment and complete the interview.

While Diane was a reporter by day, she was also taking law classes at night at the University of Louisville in Kentucky. She had enrolled in the program thinking that her career would include law, like her father, but she changed her mind after just one semester. "It's not gracious to think of law as an amusement," Diane said, "but it was a perfect antidote to what I was doing during the day. I did find the cases fascinating . . . like soap opera with a conscience."

In 1969, when Diane was 23, her father crashed his car into an abutment while driving to work one morning, and was killed. Diane was beset by grief. Later she reflected on her father's influence on her and her family, using a reference from the novel *The Unbearable Lightness of Being*:

> Milan Kundera says you can judge people by the eyes that they feel on them. Actors and actresses like the feeling of anonymous eyes. Then there are people who mainly like the feeling of all eyes in the room. Then there are the people who want to have the eyes—and the love— of only one other person. But finally there are the people who feel the need for unseen. While my father was alive, he was the reference point, the center of gravity in our family; after he died, he became the unseen eyes.

After her father's death, Diane quit her job and took a road trip with her grieving mother, Jean. The trip spurred Diane to make a change. She already had a growing interest in government and politics and had decided she didn't want to stay in Louisville. One of her father's associates suggested that she try Washington, D.C. This seemed like a logical choice. Because it was the center of politics, Diane believed that she would enjoy living there. Confident as a full-fledged reporter known for her hustle and enterprise, she decided to leave WLKY in 1970 and move to Washington, D.C., intent on finding a job there.

"I was looking for an intellectual vitamin," said Diane. "I began to feel restless. I'd lie awake at night feeling that something wasn't right. I'd wait for the revelation, the sign pointing in the direction of the Big Dream. . . . I didn't realize that . . . the dream is not the destination but the journey."

Diane moved to Washington, D.C., in 1970. When she learned that it would be some time before she could work as a CBS reporter, she headed straight for the White House, where she quickly found a job working for Ron Ziegler, the press secretary for President Richard Nixon.

Diane visited all of the television stations in Washington once she arrived. Only one extended her a job offer. Bill Small, the Washington bureau chief for CBS, had worked in Louisville and knew Diane's family. He interviewed Diane and was ready to hire the bright and eager candidate on the spot. There was just one problem: the company had a hiring freeze. Diane had to wait until a job would become available at CBS.

Not one to rest on her laurels, Diane embarked on another goal—to work at the White House. She recalled her idealistic ambitions: "Now I know this may sound incredibly naïve, but when the plane landed at National Airport, I got off with a very firm idea of where I wanted to work—at the White House. True, in the eyes of official Washington I might be right off the equivalent of the turnip truck, but working in the White House was exactly what I had in mind!"

Diane's father's career as a Republican county judge in Kentucky had given him contacts with important Republicans in Washington. One of his contacts on the Republican National Committee landed Diane an interview with Ron Ziegler, the White House press secretary for President Richard Nixon. Ziegler handled all newspaper, radio, and TV reporters, made announcements, and served as a go-between so the president wouldn't be constantly bombarded with questions and requests. Ziegler hired Diane in 1970, the halfway point in Nixon's first term.

Chief Justice Earl Warren administers the oath of office to Richard Nixon at the U.S. Capitol Building in January 1969. Diane worked at the White House during most of Nixon's presidency and later became one of his close associates.

4

THE NIXON YEARS

Diane's seemingly far-fetched idea of working at the White House became reality. Always humble, she has said that she was certain the recommendations of many of her father's friends and colleagues and their deluge of Ziegler with calls helped her land the job.

In October 1970, she became an assistant to Deputy Press Secretary Jerry Warren. At the White House, Diane started by writing press releases. In less than a year, she moved up to the position of administrative assistant to Press Secretary Ron Ziegler. She later became a staff assistant to President Nixon and had progressed to drafting some of Nixon's public statements. "[The job] was not ideological," Diane says. "I would have been just as happy working for [the Democratic presidential candidate] George McGovern." And she was happy to have a job doing what she loved to do.

Ziegler recalled that Diane Sawyer was very detail-oriented and adept at handling the tasks of her position. She and President Nixon got along well. He referred to her as "that smart girl" and "the tall girl." During her first encounter with Nixon, Diane literally ran right into him. "I was on my way to the Xerox machine, scissors in hand, and I bumped into him and knocked him down," she said. "Two Secret Service men grabbed me. The President was actually very funny about it . . . said I could get hurt that way." However, while Diane's star continued to rise, the Nixon administration was headed for trouble.

An incident that would evolve into the scandal known as Watergate occurred toward the end of Nixon's first term in office. At 2:30 A.M. on June 17, 1972, five men were arrested in the Watergate building, a luxury apartment building, hotel, and office complex in Washington, D.C. These men had broken into the headquarters of the National Democratic Committee, which was working to elect its candidate George McGovern in the upcoming presidential election. The men were wearing surgical gloves to avoid leaving fingerprints, and they were carrying electronic gear. It looked as if they had been trying to tap the phones.

At first, the major newspapers and most Washingtonians didn't treat Watergate seriously. Because Nixon was predicted to win the fall election by a landslide, there didn't seem to be any reason to steal information from the Democrats. The men who broke into Watergate were tried and convicted in U.S. District Court of conspiracy, burglary, and wiretapping in January 1973—after Nixon was reelected to the U.S. presidency. Nixon easily defeated his Democratic opponent, George McGovern, in his run for a second term as president.

Eventually it turned out that the five men had broken into the Watergate building because some members of the Nixon reelection campaign committee—the Committee to Re-Elect the President (CREEP)—had wanted to tap the phones at the Democratic headquarters. If they could listen in on the Democrats' conversations, they thought that they would acquire information to help secure a victory for Nixon in the fall election. They were also looking for papers that would show how much the

Democrats knew about campaign funds that supporters had contributed to Nixon's reelection campaign.

During the months following the Watergate break-in, disturbing facts were uncovered, many determined by *Washington Post* reporters Carl Bernstein and Bob Woodward. Among the published stories were efforts that had been made to discredit the Democratic presidential candidate, as well as tales of illegal spying, hidden funds of money, and corrupt activities at all levels of government—not just a few minor officials at CREEP. One of the Watergate burglars—James McCord—wrote a letter to Judge John Sirica, who had tried the case, charging that people in very high places in government had covered up what had happened at the Democratic Committee headquarters in the Watergate building. The accusations against the Nixon administration increased as did suspicions of a link between the burglars and the White House.

Following the events of the Nixon years, people would forever associate the Watergate office complex with the Watergate scandal of 1972, in which five men working for the president broke into the headquarters of the National Democratic Committee. Diane eventually became an expert on Watergate, and Nixon would draw from her research on the scandal when he later wrote his memoirs.

In August 1973, Nixon falsely stated in an address to the nation that he knew nothing of the Watergate events. A year later, the president would resign from office.

From the very beginning of the scandal, President Nixon kept telling the American public that he knew nothing about the Watergate events. He kept repeating that no one in his administration had been involved in the break-in, and if someone had, he, as the president, would have found out about it.

Nixon began his second term in January of 1973. In the following months he would accept the resignations of two close personal aides—H. R. Haldeman and John Ehrlichman—as their involvement in the scandal was revealed. In May, the Senate set up a special investigative committee to determine what had happened at Watergate. The Senate Select Committee on Presidential

Campaign Activities consisted of seven senators and was chaired by Senator Sam Ervin of North Carolina. The committee's televised hearings took place over the next three months, and gave the public the opportunity to evaluate for itself what had taken place within the U.S. government.

At first many Americans believed Nixon's claim that he knew nothing of the burglary or any attempts to cover it up. But as more information about secret money funds and illegal activities came to light, the public grew more and more suspicious.

In June 1973, Nixon's attorney, John Dean, who had been fired from his post at the White House in April, testified at the Senate investigation hearings. He claimed that Nixon had been involved in Watergate, and had even approved plans to pay the Watergate burglars to suppress any information that might have linked the incident to the White House.

The next month, a former White House aide, Alexander Butterfield, told the Senate committee members that a secret tape-recording system existed in the White House. Nixon had been secretly recording conversations in his office for years, with most people unaware that their conversations were routinely being recorded, according to Butterfield.

The members of the Senate committee decided that listening to the tapes would help them determine just how much Nixon had known about Watergate and when he knew it. Once he learned of the tapes, a special Watergate prosecutor, Archibald Cox, moved to have them turned over to his office. However, Nixon would not allow this, claiming "executive privilege" allowed him to keep them in the interests of national security. He also claimed that the tapes were his private property and he intended to use them for writing his memoirs after his presidency.

The battle between the White House and the special prosecutor's office to obtain the tapes reached all the way to the United States Court of Appeals. In October that court ruled that the White House had to turn the tapes over.

At around the same time, yet another scandal was taking place at the White House. Nixon's vice president, Spiro T. Agnew, resigned after being charged with accepting bribes from construction companies doing business in the state of Maryland while he served as its governor and even later when he had become vice president. President Nixon submitted the name of Representative Gerald Ford of Michigan to the Congress for confirmation as vice president. On October 12 Congress confirmed the appointment, thus making Ford the first nonelected vice president in U.S. history.

In the midst of the turmoil, several bills were introduced in the House calling for Nixon's impeachment. In an impeachment attempt, the members of the House of Representatives vote to decide if they should remove a public official from office. In the government of the United States, the House brings articles of impeachment against an official and the Senate brings the impeached person to trial. If convicted by the Senate, the official is removed from office.

Only two U.S. presidents have been impeached— Andrew Johnson and Bill Clinton. In 1868, Radical Republicans in control of the House of Representatives impeached President Andrew Johnson. He and the Congress had become adversaries soon after Johnson took office in April 1865, just at the end of the U.S. Civil War. A Southerner, Johnson had been more sympathetic toward the defeated Confederacy than the Radical Republican majority in Congress. A defiant man, he had offended congressmen who were already disturbed by the growth of presidential power that had taken place during the Civil War.

In an effort to limit the president's power, Congress had passed several laws. One of these, the Tenure of Office Act, stated that any official who had been

The only presidents besides Richard Nixon to be threatened with impeachment were Andrew Johnson (left) in 1868 and Bill Clinton in 1998–99. Congress voted to impeach Johnson but did not remove him from office. The Senate trial of Clinton failed to achieve even a simple majority for his removal.

appointed by the president with Senate approval could not be removed from office without the Senate's consent. Johnson thought the act was unconstitutional. In the summer of 1867, when he believed that Secretary of War Edwin Stanton was in effect a Radical "spy," Johnson removed him from office without seeking Senate approval. But Stanton refused to leave, barricading himself in his office and continuing to issue orders.

The Radicals decided that Johnson would have to be removed from the presidency by impeaching and convicting him of "high crimes and misdemeanors" committed while in office. In February 1868 the

House voted to impeach Johnson by submitting 11 articles of impeachment to the Senate for such crimes as Johnson's attempt to remove Stanton from office and for criticizing Congress "in a loud voice." From March through May, the president stood trial in the Senate, but when it came time for the legislative body to vote, he was not convicted. The votes fell short of the required two-thirds, and the Radicals abandoned their efforts to impeach Johnson.

More than 100 years later, President Bill Clinton would be impeached for lying about an illicit sexual affair with Monica Lewinsky, a White House intern. In October 1998, the House of Representatives voted to initiate impeachment hearings to examine allegations against Clinton of perjury and obstruction of justice. In December, the House approved, in a nearly party-line vote, two of the four articles of impeachment drafted by the House Judiciary Committee. The Senate trial opened in January 1999. The final vote taken in February of that year failed to produce even a simple majority in favor of convicting and removing the president from office.

The possibility of impeachment forced Nixon's hand in 1973, and he finally released the tapes to the new special prosecutor, Leon Jaworski. It was soon discovered that some of the tapes were missing. Some parts had even been erased. At this point, some of Nixon's aides began to privately encourage the president to step down, but he refused to resign.

In April 1974 Special Prosecutor Leon Jaworski and the House Judiciary Committee requested more tapes. They were provided instead with transcripts; some showed that Nixon did know about the Watergate cover-up.

Still, business went on as usual at the White House. In June Nixon traveled to the Middle East, and then continued on to a summit meeting in the Soviet Union.

Meanwhile, in her efforts to understand the Watergate scandal, Diane Sawyer was working overtime.

"The [White House] guards told me I had the longest hours at the White House," Diane said. As a result, she became an expert on the subject. Along with documenting the events of the scandal, she was also assigned responsibility for media coverage. Some reporters, such as Dan Rather, criticized Diane's reluctance to give the media information because she had grown close to Nixon. But at the same time, he praised her depth of knowledge on the topic, recalling, "She was a total nonsource, close to the cuff. . . . She was very competent about her job, and if you needed a statistic or a spelling at the last minute, she was always the one you went to."

In hindsight, Diane wishes she had kept notes about what went on in the White House during this time, but she had too much to do. The White House press office was always in operation. Diane remembers she was so busy that she didn't even have time to buy furniture for her apartment. "I slept on a mattress on the floor for three years," she recalls.

During the Watergate controversy, Diane stuck by Nixon, despite being bothered by the events taking place. She later noted, "I was aware there were some very troubling things going on, but I was also aware that there was a human being in a crisis situation. I am by nature loyal, and I refused to make a snap judgment."

In July the House Judiciary Committee began proceedings to impeach President Nixon for obstruction of justice, misuse of presidential powers, and refusal to comply with its request for evidence. However, on August 8, 1974, Nixon announced he would resign the office of president, and signed his formal resignation the next morning. On August 9, Gerald Ford became the 38th president of the United States. Just one month later, President Ford officially pardoned Nixon for his role in Watergate, erasing the need for a trial against Nixon.

On August 9, 1974, Richard Nixon officially ended his presidential career with a famous goodbye wave before boarding a helicopter on the White House lawn. In the following months, Diane worked with Nixon in San Clemente, California, where she served on a team making the transition between the administration of Nixon and that of the new president, Gerald Ford.

The day Nixon resigned, he boarded a plane with his family and closest advisors to his home in San Clemente, California. Diane Sawyer, who was very loyal to Nixon, was on that plane with a team of eight journalists who helped him organize the Watergate materials for his memoirs. Diane expected to stay four months to help shape the presidential papers into a manuscript, but her stint lasted four years.

"It was a human consideration," said Diane. "Here was a man whose dreams were shattered. If I didn't come through for him at a time when he needed me, I couldn't have lived with myself. . . . Here was a man who, in better times, had given me a ringside seat to a lot of history. But it wasn't just gratitude. When someone's dreams have shattered around him, and he asks you for help, what kind of person would you be if you said no?" Diane explained her decision in the simplest terms: "I had worked for this man, and he had been good to me. Now he was asking me for something I was in a position to give. I have never regretted the decision. I stayed."

Some people assumed that Diane wanted to be near Frank Gannon (Nixon's favorite speechwriter), who was also at work on the memoirs and with whom she was eventually romantically linked. But Diane denies that her decision to go to San Clemente had anything to do with Gannon. "I did not go to San Clemente to be near Frank," she said. "I barely knew him then. We'd met, but only casually. I was on the plane because the President asked me to be."

Sensing that she was part of history was another reason Diane went to California. "What could be more stimulating than to sit with a man who is the political continuity of my generation? . . . To watch him reconstruct his life and search through the past to examine the way it defined his destiny, to hear him talk about the people he met, the differences they made, and the difference they might have made. It was taxing, it was exhausting, and it was a graduate education to exceed any other."

Soon after she arrived in San Clemente, Diane served as part of the transition team from the Nixon to the Ford administration from August 1974 to July 1975. Then she took on the task of organizing the Watergate files. Finally, Diane became Nixon's research assistant and joined Frank Gannon and Ken Khachigan, another speechwriter for Nixon, in helping the former president write his autobiography, *R N*.

Part of Diane Sawyer's duties while working on Nixon's memoirs was to "read every newspaper and watch every TV report." She developed an encyclopedic knowledge of Watergate's intricacies, and, at one point, even thought she "might help the lawyers try to piece the puzzle together," she says.

Diane delved deeply into her task. She interviewed key players, including Nixon's former chief aides and Nixon himself, and created a flowchart that traced the Watergate events and players and established the links between them. "I cross-referenced everything," Diane said. "I had the definitive cross-reference dictionary of Watergate. Everything that I could think of, everything that was on the public record, I read through and reorganized in a cross-referenced, chronological book of my own."

In July 1977, when Diane showed Nixon the chart of events that she had created for Watergate, he said, "This is the first time I've understood what the hell went on."

Whenever Diane Sawyer is asked to write what she thinks about Nixon, she has said, "I've read his diaries, his letters. He is such a self-consciously private person —it comes from his Quaker upbringing. When he was a little boy, he had to ask permission to hug his brother." Diane therefore believes that writing about Nixon's private side would be a betrayal of trust.

Many dispute whether or not Diane felt more indebted to Nixon than she needed to be. She admits that she has never felt, in any way, tainted by the Watergate scandal: "That was something I watched him go through . . . and watched the country go through. We didn't know what he knew. It wasn't like a trip to the Soviet Union or the opening of China. What a considerable presidency it would have been without Watergate. But when it became clear what had happened, it was too late to be mad. It was over. His world had collapsed."

The Memoirs of Richard Nixon

"INFORMATIVE, EXPLICIT...AN IMPORTANT SOURCE FOR STUDENTS OF THE NIXON PRESIDENCY."
—THE NEW YORK TIMES BOOK REVIEW

WITH A NEW INTRODUCTION BY THE FORMER PRESIDENT

Published in 1978, RN chronicled Nixon's tumultuous and controversial presidency between 1969 and 1974. The book covered the Watergate scandal and benefited greatly from Diane's research on the topic.

Indeed, Diane views her experiences in San Clemente as a learning experience. "[I] learned a great deal about self-discipline and self-renewal. . . . I came to appreciate the way in which experience hones perception."

Once the manuscript was completed, Diane, then age 32, took a vacation in Hawaii before moving back to Washington, D.C., again her next career stop.

After her stint as Richard Nixon's assistant, Diane returned in 1978 to the world of television journalism. She began as a reporter for CBS, and within 18 months moved up to become a news correspondent.

5

BACK TO THE REAL WORLD

Many of Diane's colleagues assumed that her long-term working relationship with President Nixon would hurt her career. Diane set out to prove otherwise, but admitted that it was not an easy transition from California back to broadcast journalism.

In 1978, William Small, who had offered her a job when she first came to Washington, was able to hire her. Even as president of news at CBS, he faced many critics when he brought Diane on as a general assignment reporter with CBS's Washington bureau. "He had to fight like crazy," said Diane. "There was unilateral opposition to me at the network."

Still, Small persisted, successfully bringing Diane on board as a reporter. Her assignments were less than ideal, however. "Real drudgery—fill-in radio spots at the White House kind of thing," Diane admits. However, other reporters complained. Dan Rather, the anchor of the *CBS Evening News*, complained that Diane had no real journalistic experience—that she had simply been Nixon's loyal follower for eight years. But once again, Diane proved the naysayers wrong by working hard to prove her worth.

Within 18 months after joining CBS, Diane had moved up from the position of reporter to correspondent. The promotion resulted from her hard work on an assignment covering Three Mile Island, her first assignment for CBS.

In March 1979, the cooling system failed in the reactor of a nuclear power plant at Three Mile Island, near Harrisburg, Pennsylvania. Without the cooling system, severe core damage to the reactor occurred and a small amount of radioactive gases was released. At first, people feared that a nuclear explosion would occur. Thousands of people living nearby had to evacuate, having little time to prepare and often unable to take their belongings with them. The event caused severe psychological stress on the public, especially upon those living in the area. The crisis at Three Mile Island lasted for 12 days.

Diane covered the story in her clear, concise reporting style, which brought her to the attention of a viewing audience that up until then hadn't known who she was. She educated viewers about nuclear power and pointed out its potential for disaster.

Because of Diane's intelligent reporting and tenacious coverage of the Three Mile Island crisis, she soon earned subsequent major journalistic assignments that any reporter would consider challenging. Just six months after her promotion, Diane was assigned to cover the State Department. Her reports began appearing regularly on *CBS Morning News*. This assignment helped Diane to become a familiar face to the American viewing audience.

Diane also gained recognition for another story—the Iranian hostage crisis. In October 1979, a group of Islamic fundamentalists stormed the United States Embassy in Tehran, Iran, in the Middle East, and took 66 Americans hostage. Although 13 were released, President Jimmy Carter and the State Department had little success in trying to free the remaining 53 because

the leader of Iran, Ayatollah Khomeini, supported the fundamentalists. The hostage crisis would drag on for nearly 15 months. As she had on many assignments before, Diane showed tremendous stamina.

During the crisis, Sawyer once spent a solid week camped out at the State Department, where she could learn the latest news as soon as it became available. She often slept in chairs, although only for one or two hours at a time, when she got the chance. Diane was constantly on the phone interviewing whomever she could contact, including government officials and the families of hostages. She always seemed to be on television—in the morning, sometimes in the evening, and

One of the first major stories that Diane covered as a CBS reporter was the 1979 disaster at the Three Mile Island nuclear power plant near Harrisburg, Pennsylvania. The story alerted many Americans to the potential dangers of nuclear power, and helped make Diane a more visible figure on television.

from time to time on the *CBS News Sunday Morning* show. Hosted by television broadcast journalist Charles Kuralt, *Sunday Morning* helped Sawyer become a familiar face to the viewing public.

In the fall of 1980, after *CBS Morning News* expanded its morning shows to six days a week, Sundays through Fridays, the daily program was renamed *Morning*. Charles Kuralt took over as the daily host. During this time Diane appeared frequently on the weekday news program with Kuralt. After her reports, she remained on camera to carry on informal discussions with the host about the events taking place in the news. Because these conversations contained significant information and were filled with references to history and literature, many viewers took notice. They welcomed the serious discussions after years of being subjected to the light bantering that broadcasters often fill time with between news stories.

One person who noticed Diane's knowledge and ease in front of the camera was television broadcast journalist Mike Wallace, an early correspondent on *60 Minutes*. "I was mesmerized by her knowledge of the beat," Wallace said, "by her capacity to synthesize information in a remarkably illuminating way. You're given two minutes to tell an important story, all the work you've done all those months has got to be reflected somehow in that . . . this woman knows what she's about."

It was clear that Diane had finally shed her ties with Watergate. She was doing well as a CBS correspondent and as a regular on the *Sunday Morning Show*. Then an even bigger break came her way in 1981.

CBS network executives were pleased with the way Kuralt and Sawyer had worked together when she appeared on *Sunday Morning*. They also liked the quality of Diane's news reports during the Iranian hostage crisis.

At age 35, Diane was no longer the unseasoned neophyte in the world of broadcast news. Because the

TV anchor Charles Kuralt was a familiar face for years on CBS Sunday Morning News. *Diane made an impact on TV viewers during her first appearances with Kuralt on the show. CBS producers were so impressed with the duo that in 1981 they gave Diane a permanent position and renamed the show* Morning with Charles Kuralt and Diane Sawyer.

executives of the CBS network were impressed with her abilities, Diane was offered a coanchor spot on the *Morning* program, which had been expanded from one hour to 90 minutes in length, and renamed *Morning with Charles Kuralt and Diane Sawyer*. For Diane, this meant moving to New York City. And on September 28, 1981, she and Charles Kuralt officially began work as a team.

CBS had a strong reputation in the evening news hour; however, *The CBS Morning News* (as it was first called) just couldn't seem to compete with the other morning programs of the major networks. NBC's *Today* show and ABC's *Good Morning America* were just too strong. In efforts to boost ratings, CBS had often changed the hosts for its morning program, ultimately using 15 different anchorpersons over a 27-year period, but to no avail. CBS hoped that the ratings would finally rise now that the network had the winning combination of Kuralt and Sawyer.

Diane was thrown into one of the most difficult jobs in television—appearing daily and live. She was terribly nervous, she later recalled: "I had a half hour of exquisite agony two days before the first broadcast. But then it passed."

What a schedule! Each weekday, Diane was out of bed between 1:00 A.M. and 2:00 A.M. She arrived at the CBS studio less than an hour later. After 15 minutes of exercise, she read newspapers. This took a while; she read the *New York Times*, *New York Daily News*, *Wall Street Journal*, and *Washington Post*. She also read any news stories that had arrived overnight from wire services and from overseas news bureaus.

Next, Diane met with the news crew. Together, they discussed the morning's show, including who was to be interviewed, what stories were breaking, and who would do what. Then it was time for Diane to write. *Morning*, as it was eventually called, had staff writers, but Diane often preferred doing her own writing when she could. This way, she felt, her own words and phrasing made the stories more suited to her.

Next came the time for doing Diane's makeup and hair styling. And so, several hours after arriving at the studio, Diane went before the camera, looking alert and raring to go. Little did viewers know that she had already been hard at work for hours before appearing on camera. However, even after Diane had finished the *Morning* show, her day wasn't over. She still had calls, meetings, and interviews—often lasting until 5:00 P.M.

Diane did find time for herself. On her day off, she went to the movies, attended dinner parties, and ate meals with friends. Some of these friends included columnist Liz Smith and composer Marvin Hamlisch. On weekends, Diane saw more movies, attended plays and concerts, caught up on sleep, went shopping, read, and cooked.

Diane's busy schedule left her little time to furnish her Manhattan apartment. Neighbors in her building said her apartment resembled a "college dormitory," sparsely furnished and decorated. She had a rowing machine in her dining room. "I don't care about things," Diane said about the plainness of her new home.

There were rewards for all Diane's hard work, of course. For this busy schedule, she was paid very well. Toward the end of her stint on the news show, she was earning $800,000 a year.

After the team of Diane Sawyer and Charles Kuralt had been working together on the morning show for a year, its number of viewers had risen by 30 percent. Although the show still ranked third among the morning shows of the three major networks, *Morning* could claim a respectable share of the viewers.

Much of the credit for the show's success went to Kuralt and Sawyer. Kuralt was calm and unruffled, familiar and well liked by audiences. Therefore, he was easy to take in the morning. Diane's wit, warmth, and talents were a good match for Charles Kuralt. The *Morning* reporting team had skill and professionalism and didn't rely on glitzy sets and fancy electronic gadgets.

The show's success can also be attributed to Diane's refusal to present "soft" stories—the kind of assignments often given to female correspondents at that time. Soft stories featured fashion, human interest, and other "light" subjects. Considered fillers, they could be aired at any time. Diane spent her time instead on hard-hitting interviews and covered on-the-scene news stories.

One memorable interview of Diane's was with former president Richard Nixon, the man for whom she had worked so hard for many years. In 1982, for the 10th anniversary of the Watergate scandal, Diane had requested that her former boss participate in an interview on *Morning*. Nixon accepted and also invited her to go out for dinner later that evening. This interview was important to Diane because she could show how objective she could be even after being so involved with the former president of the United States. The interview began pleasantly enough, almost like a reunion of old friends. The two covered many subjects.

But then Diane questioned Nixon about the press and Watergate. There was some tough give-and-take during their conversation. Diane asked Nixon what Watergate now meant to him. He answered, "It happened a long time ago. I've said everything I can on the subject. I have nothing to add, and I'm looking to the future rather than the past. . . . Never look back."

Diane then countered, "But a lot of people say, and these are common people, ordinary people, people in the street, say that you never just said, 'I covered up and I'm sorry.'"

Nixon looked upset. "Well, that—is, of course, not true," Nixon replied. "As a matter of fact, if you—if you go back and . . . read my memoirs, I've covered all that in great, great detail. And I've said it all, and I'm not going to say anything more in the future."

Diane continued to press Nixon on the subject, and he grew increasingly angry. When she asked Nixon about whether he regretted not having burned the tapes that he later had to turn over to Watergate investigators, Nixon replied, "I've covered that also, of course, in my—in my memoirs, and I must say that if—I must get—I must get a—oh, a half a dozen letters a week even now. 'Why didn't you burn those tapes?'

And the answer is, of course, I should [have]. It should have been done. But the main part is, they should never have been started."

After the interview with Nixon, people questioned whether Diane was as tough on the former president as another reporter might have been. "Rougher," she replied. She said that the interview troubled her later. "It was a very tough interview, with a whole section of Watergate questions, and I wondered in the end if I was overcompensating in some subconscious way. I don't know. You never know those things." And did Diane think Nixon thought the interview was tough? "Yeah. I think he did," was her reply. In fact, when Diane returned to her office, a message was waiting for her from Nixon saying that their scheduled dinner that evening was cancelled.

Diane prepares to deliver a report for a CBS News program. Diane's audience appreciated her serious, hard-nosed journalist approach, which was a huge departure from the "soft" reporting of many other women correspondents at the time.

Despite this tense episode, Nixon and Diane remained on good terms until his death in 1994. Although they weren't what one may consider friends, they stayed in contact by phone and maintained a cordial relationship.

In 1982, Charles Kuralt left the *Morning* program, and Diane was joined by Bill Kurtis from Chicago. Diane believes that unlike the women at the ABC and NBC shows at the time, she shared responsibilities 50-50 with her male coanchor. The ratings remained good, despite Kuralt's absence, and Diane's sunny disposition and commanding delivery helped edge the network's program ratings closer to those of its rivals. Her presence and teamwork with Bill Kurtis gave CBS its first healthy ratings in this time slot in 30 years. But then the ratings began to dip.

Rumors swirled that Bill Kurtis and Diane Sawyer were not getting along with each other. Both protested otherwise. Sawyer said, "I like him very much. There was lots of laughter during the commercials." Kurtis said of the situation, "We liked each other as well as any anchors can. I enjoyed it. Diane is one tough lady."

Still, Diane received criticism. Some associates characterized her as too political, blaming her when two executive producers were fired from the show. Other critics complained that she lacked the "nonthreatening quality that viewers liked in the morning when they aren't quite awake." In a *TV Guide* article, a colleague said that Diane was "just too radiant, too brilliant."

Now a morning news veteran, Diane sought new horizons. She had her sights set on CBS's *60 Minutes*, the country's top-rated newsmagazine show. Diane saw *60 Minutes* as a challenge—to be part of what she considered one of the finest news teams in the business. As it turned out, *60 Minutes* executives had Diane Sawyer on their minds, too.

60 Minutes had gotten its start in the late 1960s as a weekly show combining journalism and show business.

In 1982, newsman Charles Kuralt left the CBS show Morning, *and Bill Kurtis (left) signed on as Diane's coanchor. By this time Diane had her sights on the show* 60 Minutes *and would only remain with* Morning *for two more years.*

During the program, the correspondents would prod and probe, trying to get to the facts and the truth of issues through what is called *confrontational journalism.* Many victims of injustice had their reputations redeemed as a result of receiving exposure on *60 Minutes* stories. The show also shed light on medical research of Alzheimer's disease and HIV/AIDS.

Diane learned that CBS executives were as interested in her joining *60 Minutes* as she was: "One day my assistant burst into my office with a bulletin. She had just heard Don [Hewitt, long-time producer of *60 Minutes*] tell a CBS seminar he hoped I would be able to join the *60 Minutes* team. He hadn't mentioned dates, but to me it seemed like the equivalent of reading in the parish notes that the pope wants to name you a cardinal. . . . I was pleased. I was honored. I was afraid it wasn't true."

To get the job, Diane had to confront Hewitt and ask for it. She recalled, "Hewitt was going around telling everybody that he wanted [Diane] Sawyer on the show, but he never told me." The suspense got to be too much for Diane. She eventually asked, "What about it, Don?"

When the CBS producer was asked why it took him so long to hire a female correspondent and why he eventually chose Diane, he exclaimed, "Sex has nothing to do with it! I would have hired her if her name was Tom Sawyer, and I want you to print that! She challenges, she moderates, she cross-examines." Another CBS producer added, "And she can flirt like mad to get the answer she wants. If a story is frothy, for example, she has fun with her subjects—she enjoys them. She's always genuinely interested."

In 1984, Diane became the first female correspondent on *60 Minutes*. (Hewitt had actually offered famed television journalist Barbara Walters a spot as the first woman on *60 Minutes* in the early 1980s, but she had turned him down.) Diane joined Mike Wallace, Harry Reasoner, Ed Bradley, and Morley Safer on the *60 Minutes* team of correspondents. Hewitt believed that Diane would blend in well with the others. "Diane was working so hard to impress me that she was the one for *60 Minutes* that she didn't notice I was working just as hard to impress her that *60 Minutes* was the one for her," said Hewitt.

Diane had worked with Ed Bradley when the two were Washington correspondents. They had also become friends. "I admire her because she went against the odds," Bradley noted. "In the beginning she went where she was not wanted and she won people over. She was that good and that sincere."

However, being the first woman to work in the male-dominated program initially proved difficult. The atmosphere at *60 Minutes* seemed hostile—Diane remembers the experience as going into "the most testosterone-packed room I had ever walked into in my life." But she won over her colleagues and critics alike with her aggressive interviewing style. Sawyer eventually received six Emmy nominations for her work on the show.

In 1984, at the height of her career, Diane signed on as a correspondent for the ground-breaking newsmagazine 60 Minutes. *Here, she poses with the rest of the* 60 Minutes *team: Morley Safer (bottom left), Ed Bradley (top left), Mike Wallace (top center), and Harry Reasoner (top right).*

Diane had the hard-hitting interview style needed for *60 Minutes.* "Sure, I'm my mother's daughter," said Diane. "I was brought up to be polite to people. But when I'm actually in the middle of an interview and I think someone is being inconsistent or not telling me the truth or thinking they can trick me, then I tend to forget my Emily Post school of journalism. I am up to the [task] as much as anyone." In fact, one CBS news producer described Diane as having "the skill of a surgeon—she gets under her subject's skin, but without drawing blood."

Indeed, Diane has been praised for her unique ability to persuade subjects to reveal information about themselves in very surprising ways. For example, she was able to tease Prince Charles of England into talking about some of his brother Andrew's misdeeds, even though it was a topic officials at Buckingham Palace had specifically ordered her not to cover. She also persuaded Lady Bird Johnson to admit that her husband, former president Lyndon Johnson, had hurt her when he had personal relationships with other women outside of their marriage.

As a *60 Minutes* correspondent, Diane constantly stayed on the go. She often flew to five different places in a given week, working on several stories at the same time. During the late 1980s, the *60 Minutes* correspondents worked on 20 to 25 stories a year and logged about 200,000 air miles to tape stories.

In an interview Diane recalled how she and her *60 Minutes* colleagues would meet to share ideas when they could synchronize their hectic schedules: "We [would] sit around and ask each other, 'Where are all the stories that have never been told? The secrets, the scandals, the corrupt practices we should be revealing?'"

When asked about her interviewing methods, Diane explained, "I like the way you can see the world in the grains of sand. I'll stop in the middle of [a] piece and show you what they have for breakfast."

And when asked what she thought about the sometimes controversial tactics *60 Minutes* would use to get answers from subjects, Diane replied, "Well, I think the ambush interview should be the interview of last resort. I mean, you have to weigh the need for tactics like that—only in a very few cases could it be justified. But *60 Minutes* is looked upon as a kind of unofficial ombudsman, a place where things can be aired, explored, and in some cases exploded." Diane's contacts with Nixon associates proved invaluable. Former staffers in the Reagan administration also took her calls without hesitation.

During her five years with *60 Minutes*, Diane interviewed important political figures such as former president George Bush, former Egyptian president Hosni Mubarak, Greek prime minister Andreas Papandreou, and British prime minister Margaret Thatcher. She profiled media mogul and creator of Cable News Network Ted Turner and author James Michener. Another notable story was an interview with Velma Barfield, the first woman to be executed in more than 20 years. Other interviews included heart-warming success or human interest stories.

One of Diane's most endearing stories was about a young boy named Mohammed in the West African nation of Mali. From 1973 to 1974, the country had suffered a terrible famine, which was followed by a severe drought in the 1980s. Diane and her crew traveled to a feeding camp, where she met Mohammed. He had learned English from engineers at the camp. The boy was thin and starving and had a clubfoot. Diane took to the boy, as did her crew.

When a *60 Minutes* viewer, Cheryl Carter-Shotts, watched a rerun of Diane's story, she, too, became taken with Mohammed. She decided to adopt the boy and bring him to the United States to live with her family in Indiana. When Mohammed arrived in the United States, Diane and her crew were on the

As a correspondent for 60 Minutes, *Diane profiled many illustrious figures, including celebrated writer James Michener, here posing with members of a New Guinea tribe he met while doing research.*

scene to document his "homecoming." With his new family, the boy's health steadily improved—he gained weight, had his clubfoot operated on, and grew taller. Diane documented his progress for *60 Minutes*. Later, the Shotts family founded Americans for African Adoptions to help expedite the adoptions of other African children.

In 1986, Sawyer's contract with CBS was up for renewal. Rumors and controversy circulated widely about what she would do. Her high-profile assignments as a correspondent on *60 Minutes* had established Diane as a national figure. Viewers admired her equally for her personality and her talents as an investigative reporter. Diane decided to stay with

CBS; she and the network signed a new five-year contract for about $1.2 million per year.

Although Diane was happy at *60 Minutes*, she yearned to become an anchor on the evening news for one of the networks. "Women are an important economic and cultural force in this country," Diane said. "I think all women look forward to the day when there's a woman as coanchor of the evening news."

A media frenzy followed Diane's 1989 move from CBS to ABC and her new show, PrimeTime Live. *In an issue of* Time *magazine—an image of which appears in this publicity shot of Diane—a cover story addressed her new $6-million contract with the question, "Is she worth it?"*

6

THE LATE BLOOMER BLOSSOMS

I n 1989, a rumor again began to circulate that Diane was leaving *60 Minutes*. This time the rumor panned out. Rejecting a $10-million offer from the Fox network, instead Diane signed a $6-million contract with ABC to fulfill her ambition of coanchoring a newsmagazine program. August 3, 1989, marked the launching of *PrimeTime Live* with coanchors Diane Sawyer and Sam Donaldson, a veteran correspondent who had covered the White House during the Reagan presidency.

The live 60-minute program was investigative and included interviews with newsmakers, including actors and political figures. Although *PrimeTime Live* received poor reviews at first, after it was refashioned, it rallied in the ratings. This turnaround was aided by Diane's interviews with Marla Maples, a former wife of real estate mogul Donald Trump, and former Soviet president Boris Yeltsin in the middle of a 1991 coup.

Diane's skills contributed to *PrimeTime Live*'s success and its distinct style. After a bumpy start, the show became known for Diane's hard-hitting investigative pieces about a variety of significant issues, such as the competency of some ultrasound technicians and doctors and their roles in the misdiagnosis of breast cancer; deadbeat fathers who refuse to pay child support; breakthrough treatment of autism; and child abuse in daycare settings. With a $7-million contract, Diane had firmly established herself as one of the highest-paid women in broadcast news.

A year earlier, Diane had taken a major step in her personal life as well. Before 1988, she had often been seen with Richard Holbrooke, an investment banker who was assistant secretary of state under former president Jimmy Carter. She had also been linked with politician Bill Bradley, whom she met and dated while both were in college, multimillionaire Mort Zuckerman, whom she also dated while at college at Wellesley, and actor-director Warren Beatty.

"She's had dozens of wonderful men dying to marry her," complained Diane's mother Jean. "I don't know what keeps her from making up her mind!" Diane came close to marrying her high-school sweetheart, with their on-again, off-again relationship. But she delayed each time the subject of marriage arose and finally said no when he began to pressure her. "I love him," she told her mother, "but he kept pushing me. I simply will not, cannot be pushed."

While Diane wanted very much to marry, she said, "I'll probably wake up one morning and say, 'This is the day. This is the day to get married.'"

Upon Diane's return from an assignment in Kuwait during *60 Minutes'* 1987–1988 season, rumors began to spread that she and Holbrooke were no longer a couple. Photos of Diane and producer-director Mike Nichols began appearing in magazines.

Nichols was born on November 6, 1931, in Berlin, Germany. He appeared in a comedy act with Elaine May at New York nightclubs, and both eventually did a Broadway show based on their routines that poked fun at social customs. Later, Nichols switched gears and picked up movie directing, making films like *The Graduate* (for which he won an Oscar for Best Director), *The Odd Couple*, *Who's Afraid of Virginia Woolf?*, and *Carnal Knowledge*. Nichols also developed a great reputation producing Broadway plays as well, earning a total of six Tony awards.

In 1987 Diane had seen Mike Nichols and although she wanted an interview with him, she initially tried to avoid him, explaining, "My face was broken out, and my hair was a mess." Although she hid behind an art exhibition in the airport terminal, he sought her out and they agreed to meet for lunch. At this time, Diane was still dating Richard Holbrooke. Nichols was separated from his third wife. Soon, Diane and Mike were inseparable. "He was so intimately, mouth-droppingly fascinating that there was no time to think about flirting," Diane said. "I just tried to keep up with him."

Soon after, they decided to marry. The fact that Nichols had already been married three times didn't deter Diane. "It's like you feel this big resounding 'Yes!' inside you," Diane said.

The couple tied the knot within the year in an intimate ceremony at Martha's Vineyard, Massachusetts, on April 29, 1988. A reception was held for 12 at the home of singer Carly Simon and her husband. Sawyer and Nichols honeymooned in Europe.

"I never could have predicted that at the somewhat geriatric age of 42, I would meet the man I finally would want to marry," Diane later said. "Now what are the odds on that? And to have it occur at the same time that I was doing the work that gave me the most freedom and happiness. Do you know what it's like to be a journalist? To be able to get up and say, 'I think I'd like to know more about this today' or 'I wonder about this person or how this works' and then go do it. How can I not feel lucky when I have the freedom to do that and the love of my life at the same time? I feel lucky every day."

Diane and Mike talked about having children at one time, but they decided against it. "It seemed like we already had a lot of children in our lives," said Nichols, the father of three children who were 11, 14, and 24 when he and Diane got married. "Diane is amazing with kids. She's someone they can say anything to, and she's there for their least popular problems."

After 13 years of marriage, the couple is clearly still very close. "She's so many different people," Nichols said. "The siren, the candy striper, the wilderness heroine. . . ."

Since marrying Diane, Mike Nichols said he stopped collecting art and doesn't care so much about material things anymore. "That's the effect that Diane has had on me," Nichols explained. "She makes you question if any of that stuff is worth the energy."

Diane said of Nichols: "He wakes up funny. It's awful. He is funny all the time." She analyzed what makes her marriage work this way: "[My husband] famously said that every marriage has to have a flower and a gardener and the great ones have people who can switch back and forth and be both, and our biggest battles are over who gets to be the flower . . . sometimes you have to go up and whack! And say it's my day to be the flower."

Mike Nichols has brought balance to Diane's life, for she herself has said she sometimes fears being consumed by her work: "Sometimes I'm afraid that my work will take over my life. But I can't help it. I am addicted to it."

In her striving for complete preparation, Diane can be considered a workaholic. "Power used for purpose is the most thrilling thing in the world that's right up there with singing show tunes," Diane said. "Real power is also about giving yourself a break and a Saturday night. I have as wholesome an attitude toward work as anyone you know. When I leave it, I leave it. I'm blue jeans, glasses, no makeup, and I just laze around the house on

As the 1990s began, Diane was leading an exciting life with her new husband, producer-director Mike Nichols, whom she married in 1988 and who appears here with Diane at a premiere for his film The Birdcage.

weekends. I feel healthy. There is a fear, though, that work will take over your life—not from workaholism, but because it's so stimulating . . . and addictive. You learn something new every day."

Diane is known as a kind, devoted, and loyal friend. She has said that gifts are her only extravagance—she loves to lavish them on her friends. Diane counts among her friends Oprah Winfrey, clothing designer Diane von Furstenberg, actress Emma Thompson, and

Despite having a full schedule, Diane remains loyal to a number of close friends, including talk-show host Oprah Winfrey, who has spoken of her great admiration for Diane.

60 Minutes correspondent Lesley Stahl. She often e-mails poetry to friends. "That's typical Diane, thinking of a way to say, 'Hey, I'm thinking of you,'" said Winfrey. "All of us look for the people who can make us better, stronger, wiser. I sit up straighter when I'm around her."

Diane is known for helping her friends deal with their problems. One grateful friend of almost 30 years, Lesley Stahl, acknowledges how Sawyer has been a big help to her: "If something's wrong, it's Diane to the rescue. Whenever I need courage with my bosses, I always call her, because I know that she will strengthen me and she has. Regularly."

Besides being very passionate about her friends,

Diane is passionate about certain issues, particularly ones dealing with children. Over the years, she has volunteered her time to fight major social problems like teenage pregnancy. She explains her views on that topic:

> I believe (teen pregnancy) is a microcosm of a lot of things that trouble us. It's at the heart of what we consider to be family values. And if we can solve this one, we can solve many others. The real issue is making sure that very young teens feel they have control over who they are. So many of these teens talk about just sliding into things. And these are life-altering things. It's really about making a decision in advance, knowing that they have the option to say yes or no.

Diane felt so committed to the issue that in 1995 she volunteered her time to do a TV special entitled "Kids Speak Out: Sex Can Wait," filmed in Detroit, Michigan. Diane helped set the show up as an informative meeting with a full panel of parents, health workers, psychologists, and teenage girls who spoke about their experiences of having children early. It was an emotional and eye-opening meeting that was lent greater significance by Diana's presence as a concerned volunteer.

Two of the most eminent journalists, former Washington Post *publisher Katharine Graham (center) and ABC anchorwoman Barbara Walters (right), converse with Diane before a women's business conference in April 1991.*

7

DOING WHAT
SHE LOVES BEST

From *PrimeTime*'s beginnings in August 1989, Diane has continued with her round-the-clock routine. She has traveled extensively around the United States and abroad to report on and investigate a wide range of topics and to interview a diverse group of newsmakers and personalities. For a ground-breaking show, she traveled to Russia for an investigation of biological weapons, a story that earned a front-page headline in *The New York Times*.

During the 1989–1990 season, Diane coanchored an unprecedented broadcast from inside the Kremlin, the historic symbol of Soviet power, and an award-winning investigative report on the plane crash of Pan Am Flight 103. She also coanchored a special live broadcast with President George Bush and First Lady Barbara Bush that toured of the first family's private living quarters in the White House.

At the start of the Persian Gulf War in 1990, Diane traveled to Egypt to interview President Hosni Mubarak and to Amman, Jordan, where she interviewed King Hussein and his

American-born wife, Queen Noor. She also reported from Kuwait on the aftermath of the war. Diane's interview with Iraqi president Saddam Hussein, conducted before the outbreak of the Gulf War, was the first televised interview he had granted to a journalist of the West in nearly a decade.

During that same season, Diane conducted the first interview with former Soviet foreign minister Eduard Shevardnadze just after his dramatic resignation. Diane was also the first American television journalist in history to conduct an interview with the head of the KGB and to tour its notorious headquarters in Moscow.

From 1990 to 1991, Diane conducted a revealing investigation exposing patient neglect and physician incompetence at a veteran's administration hospital in Cleveland, Ohio. The report prompted the secretary of Veterans' Affairs to send a team to investigate conditions at the facility. The story was also honored with an Investigative Reporters' and Editors' Award for Outstanding Investigative Reporting and a Robert F. Kennedy Journalism Citation. Diane also gained an Emmy for her ongoing coverage of the Menendez brothers scandal, which involved two wealthy California brothers who murdered their parents and were sentenced to prison.

For six months, Diane pulled additional duties as the coanchor of the ABC News newsmagazine *Day One* and substitute anchor for *World News Tonight with Peter Jennings* and ABC News *Nightline*.

Highlights of the 1992–1993 season included interviews with Cuban leader Fidel Castro, Panamanian dictator General Manuel Noriega, and President Bill Clinton and First Lady Hillary Clinton in their first television interview at home after he was elected president.

Perhaps one of Diane's most widely recognized investigative stories was an undercover investigation

into packaging and sanitary conditions at Food Lion stores, which won her an award from the Investigative Reporters' and Editors' Association and a National Headliner Award. However, problems with that story eventually resulted in a lawsuit against ABC and its parent company in 1997. Sawyer stands by the accuracy of the report, but ABC lost the suit and was told to pay a $5.5 million award to Food Lion, an amount that was eventually reduced to $315,000. Diane believes the jury voted against ABC because the reporters had misrepresented themselves on job applications (in order to get hidden cameras into the stores), not because the story was incorrect.

A hidden-camera investigation of racial discrimination,

The Kremlin (center building) is the former seat of the Russian government in Moscow, a city that saw great political upheaval with the dissolution of the Soviet Union in the early 1990s. Diane was on hand in Russia to report on the ongoing situation for PrimeTime Live. For one of those stories, she became the first American television journalist to interview the head of the KGB.

which documented the different experiences of blacks and whites in America, won Diane the Grand Prize of the prestigious Robert F. Kennedy Journalism Awards. And to top these off, an undercover investigation of daycare centers, which featured disturbing footage of unsanitary conditions and inattentive workers, won her the National Headliner Award, the Ohio State Award, and Sigma Delta Chi award.

During the 1993–1994 season, Diane tackled stories on fraud in the diamond industry, the misreading of Pap smear slides at some medical labs, age discrimination faced by prospective employees over the age of 40, and the failure of the legal system to discipline unethical attorneys. Diane demonstrated her trademark drive and determination during an attempted Soviet coup, making her way into the Russian Parliament Building and into Russian president Boris Yeltsin's office.

During the next season, Diane exposed waste and bureaucracy in public school systems, tracked outlaws who dump toxic waste in backyards, and, in a landmark investigation, sent 100 prescriptions to drugstores to show how many errors they made.

Many of Diane's stories from the 1995 and 1996 seasons exemplified her determination and investigative skills. For example, she examined life inside a maximum security prison for women, for which she spent two nights in a cell with her own camera to interview the inmates. She also investigated charges of neglect and abuse at state-run institutions for the mentally retarded and exposed unsanitary conditions in fast-food restaurants. Some of her exclusive interviews included former Los Angeles police detective Mark Fuhrman, who granted Diane his first interview following the O. J. Simpson murder trial; Sarah Ferguson, Duchess of York, who for the first time talked about her divorce from Prince Andrew and the pressures of royal life; actor Robert Downey, Jr., who

addressed his drug addiction; and actress-comedienne
Ellen DeGeneres, who discussed her homosexuality
and her family.

In June 1995, Diane captured the largest-ever audience in TV newsmagazine history by snagging an
interview with Michael Jackson and Lisa Marie Presley,
who had just become husband and wife. Although the
interview scored big ratings, some critics suggested
that ABC coddled Michael Jackson and his wife Lisa
Marie Presley, daughter of deceased rock 'n' roll star
Elvis Presley, to get the interview. Diane was also
criticized by some who claimed she had not done her
homework before the interview and that she had left

*On June 14, 1995, Diane
Sawyer held a long-awaited
interview with reclusive pop
star Michael Jackson and his
wife, Lisa Marie, daughter
of rock 'n' roll legend Elvis
Presley. Millions of people
watched the* PrimeTime
Live *episode.*

many questions unanswered. Diane admits she was "caught unaware" when Jackson said that he had been cleared of charges of child molestation, which wasn't true at the time. "I was in this position that this was an extremely flammable subject, it was live, and there was a lot of ground to cover," Diane said. "Looking back, I would have covered just one subject and it would have been the charges. You always wish things were done better or differently."

In August 1998, ABC announced that Barbara Walters and Diane Sawyer would coanchor the Sunday edition of the newsmagazine *20/20*. David Westin, then ABC News president, called the combination "a dream team for prime time newsmagazines." Westin added, "They complement each other well," referring to Diane Sawyer's expertise in undercover investigations and Barbara Walters' captivating and newsworthy high-profile interviews. "Sunday night has the highest levels of viewership of any night of the week, and 9 P.M. is the (most-watched) hour," Westin said. "That puts a lot of pressure on us to attract an audience."

Diane and Walters also each anchored another edition of *20/20* during the week. Barbara Walters remained on the original Friday edition with Hugh Downs. These added episodes of *20/20* were the result of ABC's decision in May 1998 to merge the staffs of *PrimeTime Live* and *20/20* under one franchise.

In the past, the press had categorized Sawyer and Walters as personal and professional enemies who regularly fought over stories and high-profile interviews. Yet both insisted they were friends, dismissing rumors of rivalry as gossip.

"We had really been competing all these years, so now it's wonderful that we can talk on the elevator," said Barbara Walters about working with Diane at *20/20*. "Very rarely do we conflict. For example, Elizabeth Taylor promised Diane her next interview, but I wanted to interview her for my Academy Awards-night special. So Diane said to Elizabeth, 'Let Barbara do it.'"

Of her rivalry with Barbara Walters, Diane said: "I promise you that it never, ever, ever was about Barbara or me being subsumed under *20/20*. She's a girl, that's what's fun. We're the only network anchors of a prime-time news show who can talk on the air about whether fishnet stockings keep people guessing about you and if chocolate is an aphrodisiac."

Diane has admitted to a rivalry between the two broadcasters, but she also stresses that it doesn't hinder their friendship: "We do have competitive shows. We do compete for interviews. But, I also compete with Ted [Koppel]. I also compete with Peter [Jennings]. I compete with anybody who's in the race. Barbara and I do more to maintain a real friendship and camaraderie than a lot of other people in rivalrous relationships. Unfortunately, we will never escape the gossip. Somebody said once when it comes to a woman, the thing that will be believed is whatever is easiest to believe. And that's what we're up against. We're up against this plot. But the answer is I love her and I am proud to be at the same network as Barbara Walters."

Over the years, Diane Sawyer has produced insightful, hard-hitting, thought-provoking, and timely stories at *20/20*. One memorable interview she conducted was with 6-year-old Elian Gonzalez.

In November 2000 Elian Gonzalez, nearly drowned, was found by fishermen off the coast of Florida. He had been on a small boat with his mother and 12 other Cubans, as the group attempted to flee from Cuba. Besides Elian, only two other adults survived; the rest had drowned, including Elian's mother. For several months a tug-of-war over custody of the little boy ensued between his father back in Cuba and relatives of his mother in Miami.

In March 2001, Elian's Miami relatives allowed

One of the biggest stories of 2000 was that of six-year-old Elian Gonzalez, a Cuban refugee caught in a custody battle between family members living in the United States and in his native country. Diane had the chance to interview the boy shortly before U.S. authorities returned him to his father in Cuba.

Diane to spend two days with the boy. She was accompanied by a Spanish-speaking psychiatrist. During the interview, Elian spoke through an interpreter, explaining what had happened. He remembered the boat capsizing and sinking. He remembered being placed in an inner tube and, exhausted from trying to stay afloat, falling asleep. He said he was helped by dolphins and didn't wake up until he was rescued by fishermen. Elian also seemed confused about what exactly happened to his mother. "My mother is not in heaven, not lost," the boy said. "She must have been picked up here [in] Miami somewhere. She must have lost her memory, and just doesn't know I'm here." Elian also drew a picture of a boat and high waves to describe the tragedy. "Water came in," he explained.

In the end, the courts ruled that Elian should be returned to his father in Cuba. Yet his Miami relatives resisted. Finally U.S. marshals stormed their house and retrieved the boy. Eventually, Elian was returned safely to his father, a short time after Diane's interview.

Another significant interview took place with the 2000 presidential candidate Al Gore. On the day he announced his candidacy, Al Gore, accompanied by his wife, Tipper, talked candidly for the first time about his vision of a Gore presidency, his relationship with Bill and Hillary Clinton, and his feelings about the Monica Lewinsky scandal, in which Bill Clinton had a sexual relationship with a White House intern. Diane asked Gore about President Clinton's behavior and his view of the president's morality.

> *Sawyer*: Yes or no? Did Bill Clinton compromise the dignity of the presidency, with what he did with Monica Lewinsky?

> *Gore*: Yes; but I think he recovered from it. I think that it was a horrible, difficult year for the country to go through. For those of us who are his friends, we were disappointed. He suffered—unfortunately, his family also did, and others involved with that matter.

Diane went on to ask Gore about Clinton's denial to the American television audience that he ever had any sexual relationship with Lewinsky, when, later on, he admitted to a relationship with her.

> *Sawyer*: Did you believe him at that point?

> *Gore*: Ah, I didn't like that moment at all. But in, in addressing what you call a mystery about what my feelings were, I want you to understand that there shouldn't be any mystery: I thought it was awful. I thought it was inexcusable. But I made a commitment to serve this country as vice president . . . and I'm not going to turn my back on that commitment.

In March 2001, Diane interviewed Jerri Nielsen, M.D., the physician whose dramatic story of her discovery of breast cancer, self-treatment, and survival at the South Pole made headlines worldwide. Dr. Nielsen had left her job in Ohio to take a year's sabbatical at the National Science Foundation's Amundsen-Scott South Pole Station in Antarctica, one of the most remote and perilous places on earth. Those living at the research station live in almost total darkness for six months of the year, in winter temperatures as low as 100 degrees below zero. There is no way to leave or get access to the station during the winter months.

Soon into her tenure, Dr. Nielsen noticed a lump in her breast. Her health rapidly deteriorated. The segment showed Dr. Nielsen performing a biopsy on herself with the help of a welder (whom she trained by cutting vegetables!). The results were sent via satellite to the United States and diagnosed as an extremely aggressive form of breast cancer. Nielsen enlisted the help of team members to start IV lines and mix chemotherapy. Through it all, Dr. Nielsen still functioned as team doctor and team member. A daring rescue was staged by the Air National Guard, which landed, dropped off a replacement physician, and, minutes later, took off with Dr. Nielsen.

These days, as coanchor of *Good Morning America* Diane's main competition is *Today*'s Katie Couric. Diane appreciates her rival's abilities: "Katie has a really quick sense of humor, she's good at questioning, and—she'll hate me for this—but she's just so cute!" Diane also feels more than up to the task of giving Couric significant competition.

Charles Gibson, her *Good Morning America* coanchor, thinks Diane may stay on the show longer than he will. "She really likes it," he said. "She lives an extremely protected life, but her empathy for people is genuine. And she genuinely enjoys children. She covers virtually every multiple birth in America."

Even Diane's friends tend to agree that the show suits her. *Good Morning America* provides her with a platform to show her softer side, they say. "People think she's aloof, but Diane is funny as hell," said friend and talk show host, actress, and film producer Oprah Winfrey.

Whatever is next for Diane Sawyer, it is sure to attract attention to the media star, who is ambitious and a tremendously energetic go-getter. She has always been a determined, driven woman. And as a formidable television news veteran, Diane has some profound thoughts on the business of network news.

"Everybody always thought that women . . . would start to jockey for positions and women would start to edge out other women, and that we somehow felt there was a finite number and we had to make sure that we were the triumphant one," said Diane. "And the opposite happened. The opposite happened, which is, women started going and closing the door and saying, 'Oh God, let's talk.' And we did the most confounding thing of all, which is defy the plot that we were all cast in."

Diane and fellow Good Morning America *team member Lara Spencer lead off a karaoke contest on a June 28, 2001, episode. Diane's friends believe that* Good Morning America— *less serious in tone than her newsmagazine shows—helps bring out her softer side.*

It is astoundingly clear that after 35 years in television, Diane Sawyer still savors the joy of being a journalist:

[Real power] is the power to hurl an idea out into the world that can actually leave a change. That can make somebody say, either, their heart has been moved, or there will no longer be any tolerance for some injustice that there was tolerance for the day before. I love the entire process of asking questions about a story and deciding which questions matter most. What is the REAL story? What is that little detail—what shirt he was wearing, why her hair looked so bad—that helps us focus. Great questions make great reporting. Then after the research is done, I come back in for the interviews and writing. In magazine work, we get to go after the stories that we are passionate about. There are too many great and important stories only to do good and ho-hum ones. For instance, once I got a mammogram. So I decided to ask questions . . . and we had a big investigation and changed the laws. If you're curious, you'll probably be a good journalist because we follow our curiosity . . . like cats.

Diane added: "I think television is brave—that unruly combination of words and pictures exciting each other. Also, I like talking. (I didn't know at the time I would have to worry so much about my hair.) [The most fun part about my job] is getting paid to learn things. Getting to walk into the lives of people you've never met and ask them anything. Why did you commit that crime? What are you doing with your life? What can you teach us? I simply love the newness of the people, the places, the answers every day."

On breaking into the television journalism business, Diane gave one interviewer these insightful words:

My advice is to follow what you are genuinely passionate about—history, consumer work . . . and let that guide you to your destination. Maybe you want to be a sports reporter . . . or a specialist in health issues. Learn a lot about what you would want to know anyway. And then start in a small TV station so you can make all of your embarrassing mistakes early and in front of fewer people! And don't worry about the embarrassing mistakes . . . we've all humiliated ourselves over and over!

In control, totally prepared, earnest, and nice. These are adjectives routinely used to describe Diane Sawyer. But always provoking controversy, she's also been

On February 10, 1998, Diane Sawyer was inducted into the Academy of Television Arts and Sciences, along with other prominent figures in the television field. Diane has also racked up 11 Emmy awards and 31 nominations over the span of her career.

described as a gorgeous operator and the wood nymph with a microphone. She went from being a novice reporter for CBS earning $30,000 a year to the first woman correspondent at *60 Minutes* with a $1-million contract. Her swift rise as an on-air personality and news correspondent is unprecedented.

Along the way, Diane has won 11 Emmys and has been nominated 31 times. She's also accumulated such prestigious awards as the Alfred I. DuPont-Columbia University Award, the Grand Prize of the Premier Investigative Reporters' and Editors' Association, the George Foster Peabody Award for Public Service, the IRTS Lifetime Achievement Award, and the USC Distinguished Achievement in Journalism Award. She also was recognized for her accomplishments at the Spirit of Achievement ceremony hosted by the New York Chapter of the National Women's Division of the Albert Einstein College of Medicine of Yeshiva University. In 1997 she was inducted into the *Broadcast* magazine Hall of Fame and Academy of Television Arts and Sciences.

Indeed, this "dorky wallflower" has truly blossomed and has successfully climbed her way to the top with a combination of intelligence, drive, warmth, and desire to be the best.

CHRONOLOGY

1945   Born Lila Diane Sawyer to Jean W. Dunagan and Erbon Powers Sawyer on December 22 in Glasgow, Kentucky

1963   Wins the Junior Miss Contest; graduates from Seneca High School in Louisville, Kentucky

1967   Graduates with a B.A. in English from Wellesley College in Wellesley, Massachusetts; works as a reporter and weather person at WLKY in Louisville

1969   Father, E. P. Sawyer, is killed in a car accident

1970   Moves to Washington, D.C., and lands a job at the White House

1972   Watergate scandal begins receiving media coverage

1974   President Richard Nixon resigns. Sawyer goes to San Clemente, California, to help write his memoirs

1978   Returns to Washington, D.C., to work as a general assignment reporter for CBS

1979   Covers Three Mile Island nuclear reactor crisis; is promoted to correspondent for CBS

1981   Signs on as coanchor for *CBS Morning News* with Charles Kuralt. Program is later renamed *Morning with Charles Kuralt and Diane Sawyer*

1982   Interviews former president Nixon for the *Morning* show

1984   Becomes first female correspondent on *60 Minutes*

1986   Signs new CBS five-year contract for about $1.2 million

1988   Marries director Mike Nichols on April 29; is honored at 34th annual Spirit of Achievement ceremony; serves as panelist for the Reagan-Mondale presidential debate

1989   Signs on to coanchor ABC's *PrimeTime Live* with Sam Donaldson

1990   Wins Emmy for Outstanding Investigative Journalism for coverage of "Pan Am Flight 103" story (*PrimeTime Live*)

1991   Wins Emmy for Outstanding Coverage of a Continuing New Story for "Murder in Beverly Hills" (*PrimeTime Live*), a report on the Menendez brothers' trial

1996   Wins Emmy for Interview/Interviewer(s) (segments) for "McNamara's War" (*PrimeTime Live*)

1997   Is inducted into the Television Hall of Fame

1998   Starts as coanchor of Sunday edition of *20/20* with Barbara Walters
        and the Wednesday edition with Sam Donaldson

1999   Starts as coanchor of *Good Morning America* with Charles Gibson

2000   Covers the story of Cuban refugee Elian Gonzalez; between
        Diane's first day as coanchor and March, *Good Morning
        America*'s audience grows by 1.1 million

TELEVISION APPEARANCES

1967–70	*WLKY-TV* (reporter)
1978–81	*CBS Evening News* (correspondent)
1981–84	*CBS Morning News* (coanchor)
1982–84	*CBS Early Morning News* (coanchor)
1984–89	*60 Minutes* (correspondent and coeditor)
1989	*ABC News* Special: "Behind Kremlin Walls" *ABC News* Special: "Inside the White House"
1989–	*PrimeTime Live* (coanchor)
1990	*Day One*
1991	*ABC News* Special: "Murder in Beverly Hills"
1998	*20/20* (coanchor)
1999–	*Good Morning America* (coanchor)

BIBLIOGRAPHY

Blue, Rose, and Joanne E. Bernstein. *Diane Sawyer: Super Newswoman.* Hillside, N.J.: Enslow, 1990.

Bosworth, Patricia. "Diane Sawyer Makes News." *Ladies Home Journal,* February 1985.

Bowmen, J.S., ed. *The Cambridge Dictionary of American Biography.* Oxford, United Kingdom: Cambridge University Press, 1995.

Dorsey, Tom. "Lifetime Offers a Personal Glimpse of Diane Sawyer." *The Courier-Journal,* 19 February 2001.

Gerosa, Melina. "Diane Day & Night." *Ladies Home Journal,* October 1999.

Hamilton, Kendall. "Good Morning, Diane: ABC's sliding breakfast show gets a wake-up call." *Newsweek,* 18 January 1999.

Hass, Nancy. "Broadcast Muse." *Harper's Bazaar,* December 1999.

Howard, Margo. "Diane Sawyer." *People Weekly,* 5 November 1984.

Johnson, Beth. "Sisters." *Good Housekeeping,* June 2000.

Keenan, Marney Rich. "The Prime of Diane Sawyer: ABC's $6-million anchor." *The Detroit News,* 5 October 1995.

Nold, James, Jr. "We Knew Them When." *Louisville Magazine,* 1999 City Guide.

Nord, Thomas. "Wake-Up Call." *The Courier-Journal.* 13 February 2000.

Orecklin, Michele. "People: There She Was." *Time,* 5 July 1999.

"Sawyer Resetting Her Alarm Clock." *USA Today,* 8 January 1999.

"Sawyer-Walters Team for *20/20.*" *Variety,* 7 August 1998.

Yater, George H. "Louisville." *Louisville Magazine,* March 2000.

Zoglin, Richard, and William Tynan. "Good Morning, Diane." *Time Canada,* 18 January 1999.

FURTHER READING

Books and Periodicals

Auletta, Ken. "Promise Her the Moon." *The New Yorker*, 14 February 1994.

Unger, Arthur. "Diane Sawyer: 'The Warm Ice Maiden.'" *Television Quarterly*, Spring 1992.

Websites

ABC News
http://www.abcnews.go.com

Good Morning America
http://www.abcnews.go.com/Sections/GMA

MBCNet—"Diane Sawyer: U.S. Broadcast Journalist"
http://www.mbcnet.org/ETV/S/htmlS/sawyerdiane/sawyerdiane.htm

Mr. Showbiz News—"Diane Sawyer: Credits"
http://mrshowbiz.go.com/people/dianesawyer/content/credits.html

Oxygen.com—"Who Does She Think She Is?"
http://befearless.oxygen.com/features/who_ds.html

INDEX

INDEX

PICTURE CREDITS

Gerda Gallop-Goodman holds a B.A. in news editorial journalism from the University of North Carolina at Chapel Hill. She is the managing editor of a consumer health magazine in Philadelphia, Pennsylvania, and is also a freelance writer. She is the author of *Crimes Against Women* for Chelsea House's Crime, Justice, and Punishment series, and lives in Philadelphia.

Matina S. Horner was president of Radcliffe College and associate professor of psychology and social relations at Harvard University. She is best known for her studies of women's motivation, achievement, and personality development. Dr. Horner has served on several national boards and advisory councils, including those of the National Science Foundation, Time Inc., and the Women's Research and Education Institute. She earned her B.A. from Bryn Mawr College and her Ph.D. from the University of Michigan, and holds honorary degrees from many colleges and universities, including Mount Holyoke, Smith, Tufts, and the University of Pennsylvania.